Guide to Inner Wellness

Atul Sehgal is an engineering professional who has held senior positions in the power sector both in the Government of India as well as the private sector. He is also a passionate freelance writer with seven published books to his credit. Three of these are on the subject of motivation and spirituality. He has a long association with the Arya Samaj and is a keen proponent of Vedic ideology. As an author, he draws inspiration and ideas from the core philosophy of the Vedas. His last book, *The Essence of Bhagwad Gita: 70 Verses at Its Core* was a highly acclaimed work and was a unique exposition of the Bhagwad Gita, based on Vedic analysis.

He also has numerous published articles on the subject of motivation, spirituality and philosophy. Many of these articles were published by *Hindustan Times*, *New Indian Express* and *The Times of India*.

Sehgal is of the strong belief that most problems of contemporary existence stem from dilution and violation of the principles of progressive and peaceful living prescribed by the Vedas, and that solutions need to be devised accordingly.

He lives in New Delhi.

He can be contacted at: atul4956@gmail.com

Praise for the Book

Yet another unique piece of work by Sh. Atul Sehgal, this book is an analytical and pure Vedic guidance on how to attain peace, both inner and outer, for inner wellness. *Your Guide to Inner Wellness* has a remarkable set of interpretations and explanations of Vedic hymns that are relevant to stress alleviation.
—**Arya Ravi Dev Gupta**, President, Ekal Vidyalaya Foundation of India, Gen. Secretary, Ved Sansthan, Rajouri Garden, President, Arya Samaj, Safdarjang Enclave

This book touches upon crucial human problems of modern life; problems that generate tension, disharmony and stress. It also provides practical solutions drawn directly from the timeless Vedic texts. A blueprint to solve the peace-disruptive problems of the twenty-first-century world, this book is a must-read for all age groups.
—**Rtn. Suresh Bhasin,** District Governor, Rotary International District 3011

This book will help present-day humans to overcome stress, so much in evidence today. It contains valuable ideas and suggestions gleaned from the eternal divine texts—the Vedas—to establish peace. The global society and global institutions need this guidance more than ever before to realize a safer and better world for the future generations.
—**Yogesh Munjal,** Chairman and Managing Director, Munjal Showa Limited, Patron, Arya Samaj, Greater Kailash-1

This book highlights the root causes of the ills plaguing the modern generation that is ridden by doubt, confusion, tension and fear psychosis as well as provides appropriate cures to rectify them. Very interesting and thoughtful indeed, this book comes at a time of a global crisis when (or where) it is needed the most.
—**Sadhvi Dr Uttamaa Yati,** International Vaidic Missionary President, Sarvadeshik Arya Veerangana Dal

Atul Sehgal's profound understanding of the Vedic texts and worldly wisdom will inspire you to decode and apply this new-age blueprint to achieve inner peace through harmony, stability and peace at the personal and global level.
—**Ravi Shankar**, Senior journalist and author

Guide to *Inner Wellness*

ATUL SEHGAL

Published by
Rupa Publications India Pvt. Ltd 2021
7/16, Ansari Road, Daryaganj
New Delhi 110002

Sales centres:
Allahabad Bengaluru Chennai
Hyderabad Jaipur Kathmandu
Kolkata Mumbai

Copyright © Atul Sehgal 2021

All rights reserved.

No part of this publication may be reproduced, transmitted,
or stored in a retrieval system, in any form or by any means,
electronic, mechanical, photocopying, recording or otherwise,
without the prior permission of the publisher.

The views and opinions expressed in this book are the author's own and
the facts are as reported by him which have been verified to the extent
possible, and the publishers are not in any way liable for the same.

ISBN: 978-93-89967-85-2

First impression 2021

10 9 8 7 6 5 4 3 2 1

The moral right of the author has been asserted.

Printed at Gopsons Papers Ltd, Noida

This book is sold subject to the condition that it shall not,
by way of trade or otherwise, be lent, resold, hired out, or otherwise
circulated, without the publisher's prior consent, in any form of
binding or cover other than that in which it is published.

*In the memory of my mother Pushpa Sehgal,
who provided spiritual indoctrination to me*

Contents

Foreword ix
Preface xi

1. Prayer for Peace, Prosperity and Protection — 1
2. Mundane Instruments of Human Welfare — 7
3. Incantations for Happiness and Well-Being — 15
4. Peace Promotion through Preceptors and Individual Conduct — 22
5. Flow and Intensity of Nature's Elements — 29
6. Indra, Varun and Rudra: The Harbingers of Peace — 34
7. Peace Enhancement through Elements of Yagya — 40
8. Vibes of Peace from Terrestrial Elements and Spatial Directions — 46
9. Peace through Learned Folks and the Almighty — 51
10. Protection from the Radiant Sun; Beneficence from the Rulers — 56
11. Peace from Knowledge, from Devatas — 61
12. Peace from Judiciary, Skilled Men and Parents — 67
13. Happiness from the Creator; Peaceful Navigation through the Oceans — 73
14. Grace of Lord Indra for Peace and Joy — 79
15. Moderation in Flow of Primal Elements — 84
16. Prayer for Success, Preservation and Lasting Peace — 89

17. God's Blessings for Happiness and Fulfilment of Desires	94
18. Comprehensive Prayer for Inner and Outer Peace	99
19. Prayer for Longevity, Health and Freedom	105
20. Noble Aspirations for the Wandering Mind	111
21. Tame Your Mind: Set Righteous Thoughts in It	116
22. The Basis of Intelligence, Memory and Knowledge	121
23. The Prime Tool of Yogic Practice	126
24. The Key Instrument of Knowledge Acquisition	131
25. Noble Thoughts for the Restive and Ageless Mind	136
26. Health and Happiness from Meditation on God	142
27. Vibes of Fearlessness from Ether and Earth	147
28. Freedom from All Fear: Day and Night	152
Epilogue	157
Acknowledgements	159

Foreword

Mr Atul Sehgal has been writing extensively on the subjects of religion and philosophy for many years. His long and intensive association with the Arya Samaj has developed in him a passion to delve deep into the meaning of the divine mantras of the Vedas and provide an intelligible exposition of these mantras for the masses.

This book deals with the most important subject of inner wellness. The author has rightly picked up the 28 Shanti Karanam mantras from the Vedas to guide the reader on the way to attaining internal peace. The present world is stricken with stress, which takes various forms. Technology has brought more comforts and convenience to humanity, but not really helped to alleviate stress. In some sections of the present global population, new types of peace-undermining issues have erupted. This definitely throws up the need to revisit the eternal guiding philosophy of the Vedas.

Mr Sehgal has done an excellent work in delineating and describing not only the plain meaning of the 28 Vedic mantras, but also charting the way to their application in our daily life. They are, no doubt, a perfect prescription for the ills of the modern society that have generated mental stress and undermined human happiness. This book addresses the matter of human peace rather comprehensively and serves as a useful practical guide to the establishment of inner peace and wellness for the common man.

I compliment the author once again for his efforts

and recommend this book as a most useful guidebook for improving the quality of human life.

10 April 2020

Dr Dharam Pal Arya,
President, Delhi Arya Pratinidhi Sabha
(Delhi Arya Representatives Council)
15, Hanuman Road,
New Delhi 110001

Preface

Human beings are imperfect. We have limited physical strength, limited sensory power and limited mental capacity. Our intellectual prowess—the capacity to understand and absorb—is also grossly limited. Our knowledge and understanding remain incomplete. That our knowledge level is too little is best exemplified by the fact that we hardly know who we are, where we came from and where we have to go. We are at a loss to understand these very basic and fundamental facts of life.

We harbour a multitude of desires, but are hamstrung by serious knowledge gaps that hinder the fulfilment of those desires. Life is uncertain and the future unpredictable. This makes us insecure. The pressures of modern living exacerbate our sense of insecurity and stress us even further. That is where comes the necessity and role of a higher beneficent power who is our creator. The creator knows his creation best. Only He can resolve the problems of the entities created by Him. Call Him by any conceivable name—God, the Almighty, Ishwar, Allah, et al. He remains the preceptor, the sustainer and the protector of the sentient living being. He is the source of life and energy and all beneficence. He is also the source of all knowledge. He is our true friend, philosopher and guide. He is in fact the emancipator of man. The relationship between man and his Creator God is all-encompassing and eternal, as both human soul and God are immortal and eternal entities. The big difference however is that the human soul is finite and has a local, terrestrial existence, whereas God is infinite, existing throughout the vast visible universe and beyond it.

In order to lead a fulfilling life, one seeks knowledge and protection and both come from the realm of the Almighty, the latter being omniscient and omnipotent. The knowledge needed by one to lead a happy, healthy and fulfilling life, realizing his/her desired goals and objectives, has to come from his/her Creator. It cannot come from other humans, as they are all of grossly limited knowledge and understanding. This knowledge is required to overcome sorrow and attain happiness—the ultimate human goal. This knowledge refines human character and makes him/her capable of realizing his/her ambitions gradually and progressively. This knowledge, quite logically, has to come from the Creator of human beings because only the Creator knows His creation completely and well. And this knowledge, by the same logic, has to be delivered to the earliest humans at the onset of creation for transmission to their succeeding generations. This is the knowledge enshrined in the Vedas, which eternally guides humankind through the ages and eons.

When we deal with the mundane subject of 'inner wellness', we have to understand that inner wellness is just another name for inner peace, which comes from knowledge and fulfilment. Modern life is very stressful—there is little doubt in this. If, in spite of advanced 'scientific' achievements and systems of the twenty-first century, there is so much stress, violence, crime, corruption, disease and fear psychosis in the world, something is definitely amiss. We surely have knowledge and understanding gaps that erode peace and prevent progress. This book examines this particular problem, or rather impediment, to achieving inner peace. It goes with the logical and even widely accepted presumption that the Vedas are the repositories of all divinely revealed knowledge coming from our Creator. They are the universal and eternal texts of true core knowledge. The Rig Veda manuscripts have been selected for inscription in UNESCO's Memory of the World's Register, 2007.

Taking the strands of that Vedic knowledge, this book analyses the reasons behind today's high levels of mental stress and suggests appropriate measures for its alleviation. It provides a broad framework that is drawn from the backdrop of Vedic hymns for the establishment of inner peace and harmony.

The purpose of this book will be well-served if the messages presented in it are applied and followed by individuals as well as communities dispersed across the globe for promoting peace. True progress can only occur on the foundation tripod of knowledge, perseverance and practise of faith, and the term 'practise of faith' here connotes communion with the Almighty. Inner wellness and peace form an important requisite for human progress since perseverance is not possible without inner peace. Hence, this work serves a dual purpose; it guides humanity on the way to inner peace and concurrently prepares a human for his/her material and spiritual progress in real terms.

The strands of divine knowledge are very simple. But we humans, out of our intellectual limitations, tend to make simple things complicated. The primordial texts of fundamental knowledge—the Vedas—contain hymns that provide the basic truths in cryptic and coded form. They appear to be abstract and esoteric. However, with a logical approach and unbiased mind, the meaning of these hymns can be correctly deciphered and expounded. The issue of peace is most fundamental to human existence and will remain so because we seek the fulfilment of our desires and to overcome all sorrow. Inner peace and wellness remain the cornerstone of human striving, progress and salvation. This book provides a tool to achieve exactly that.

ONE

Prayer for Peace, Prosperity and Protection

Aum shannah Indragni bhavatamavobhi, shannah Indra Varuna ratahavya! Shamindra Soma suvitayashanyo, Shannah Indra Pushana vajasatau.

(O our protector, Indra; the bestower of all beautiful things, Agni Dev; the god of peace, Varun Dev; and the giver of success, Som Dev and Pushan! Bestow on us prosperity, peace and protection.)

RIG VEDA 7.35.1

This hymn of the Rig Veda is an invocation to almighty God for prosperity, peace and protection. These three things are concomitant—they cannot exist in isolation. The existence of one is dependent on the other two. The terms 'Indra', 'Agni', 'Varun', 'Som' and 'Pushan' are attribute names of the one and only God.

Indra means the one whose opulence exists everywhere. Agni is the embodiment of knowledge, omniscient and worthy of attainment and worship. Varun refers to that who is noblest, while Som connotes the immortalizing Lord. Pushan is that who carries souls to their next appropriate destination. All these names of almighty God signify His different functional attributes. They hold significance in bestowing peace, prosperity and protection on God's human subjects.

It follows from above that prosperity and protection are the prerequisites of peace. Inner wellness is the state of inner peace. Peacefulness is a condition of the heart, which is believed to comprise four parts: conscious mind, intellect, subconscious mind and ego. Peace, in this space called the 'heart', signifies and creates what is termed 'inner wellness'. But the point is: what is peace? Is the meaning of peace well understood?

'Peace' is a word with many associations. The original Sanskrit equivalent of the term 'peace' is 'shanti', which stands for calmness, harmony and purity. Hence, peace means all the three things. It is that state when your mind is calm, and you are free from tension, worry, anger and fear. In that condition, your intellectual faculty is also composed, meaning thereby that you are able to think clearly and rationally. That enables you to make sound judgments and good/wise decisions which, in turn, lead to peace in day-to-day life.

But where do harmony and purity enter the definition of peace? In the context of a person's inner wellness, harmony means the healthy relationship with others. The kind of relationship that exists between a person and his/her family members, peers, colleagues, employer, employees, neighbours or relatives determines his/her inner wellness in a big way.

Do not let the behaviour of others destroy your inner peace.
—DALAI LAMA

Harmony also means a healthy and positive attitude towards things and circumstances in a person's life. This is the attitude that generates a feeling of contentment or satisfaction.

In many situations, you may be intellectually aware and conscious about the right course of action, but if your mind is not in sync with the intellect, it may pull your thought process in an entirely different direction that may not be right or proper. In fact, the intellect faculty lies at a higher plane than the mind and should ideally control it, taking the latter along with it. If that happens, inner harmony prevails and establishes a situation for right action on your part—action that produces favourable results for your success, happiness and progress.

The above brings us to the other important component of peace—purity. Purity connotes wholesomeness and homogeneity of air, water and food. The concept extends to the mind, the intellect and the ego. The purity of these entities can be vitiated by wrong habits and, most importantly, wrong thinking. It derives from untruth and half-truths and these are abundant in today's world.

> *It isn't enough to talk about peace. One must believe in it. And it isn't enough to believe in it. One must work at it.*
> —ELEANOR ROOSEVELT

Having dealt with the exposition of the term 'peace', it is necessary to explain how prosperity and protection influence it.

Human beings innately seek perfection. They need to attain success in their mundane endeavours. They need to fulfil their basic material needs and over and above that, derive the satisfaction of worldly success. They need to become prosperous to first fulfil their basic needs and then to achieve self-actualization. A pauper can never be at peace with his/her surroundings or with himself/herself. That is why; the above hymn of the Yajur Veda contains the word 'prosperity'. Here, prosperity is not limited to money or wealth. It also connotes the sense of fulfilment or contentment. A rishi or a sage owns nothing, he has no house or money. But what he has is far greater—contentment; he is at peace with himself and the world. This is the deeper meaning of prosperity and wealth that the mantra conveys.

To become prosperous, a person has to strive and persevere. To persevere, one needs to have a healthy mind and a healthy body. One needs to have a composed intellect. A healthy mind is that which is calm and peaceful. When you are peaceful within and not gripped by attachments and greed, you will persevere without craving for reward and that is the right way forward in life to prosperity.

Submit to God and be at peace with him; in this way prosperity will come to you.

—BIBLE

That brings us to the last term in our discussion—protection. Human beings lead a very fragile existence indeed. They have the innate instinct of self-protection and preservation, but are not competent enough to handle everything. In fact, one's worldly existence is ephemeral—almost like that of the fresh morning dew drop that lies perched on a leaf and can be blown away in seconds by any surge of wind or the slightest of touch. So, one needs divine protection—from the same all-powerful entity that created him/her. That explains the significance of the term 'protection' in this hymn. Without protection or perceived protection, a person will be afflicted with fear and doubt. Absence of fear is crucial to inner wellness. And unless there is absence of inner fear and inner doubt, there can be no proper striving for prosperity;

there is no possibility of positive and affirmative action for material success and accomplishments. Who can we go to for protection then? Here comes the understanding of the all-powerful. Without being consciously and subconsciously aware of divine protection, we cannot overcome fear and hence cannot take even calculated risks. And without taking risk, we cannot grow and prosper. If we think, as some of us do, that we can independently get the better of fear and failure—without divine help, we are mistaken.

They who can give up essential Liberty, to obtain a little temporary Safety, deserve neither Liberty nor Safety.
—BENJAMIN FRANKLIN

We should get the concept of the Creator right, as the omnipotent protector and preserver. We should learn to lean on Him. That will go a long way in assuaging our stress levels. Invocation of Indra will enhance our prosperity; invoking Agni will refine our intellect and increase our knowledge-acquiring capability. Invoking Som will reduce our mental stress and fear. Invocation of Pushan is bound to help us steer our life boat in the progressive direction, bringing us success.

You're safe not because of the absence of danger, but because of the presence of God.
—ANONYMOUS

Vedic mantras are divine and work to refine our body, mind and intellect. In this way, the Self is prepared for a greater understanding of the value of the things that sustain us—the elements of Nature that mankind would otherwise have taken for granted. Only when the mind is prepared to accept and acknowledge the value of these things can we find both outer and inner well-being, which is the source of happiness.

Regular chanting of this mantra enhances peace, protection and prosperity. How does this happen? The interface between the human soul and the supersoul God is the human mind. It is the human mind that is influenced and shaped by the power of this mantra. Vedic mantras are divinely revealed. They carry great potency and power. And the human mind too is a very powerful tool. When the power of the mantra combines with the power of the mind, the mantra power is unleashed for human growth and happiness. Since God is the source of all human bounties, these Vedic mantras that come directly from God are verily the instruments of tapping His beneficence.

TWO

Mundane Instruments of Human Welfare

Aum shannobhagah shamunashanso astu shannah purandhi shamusanturaya. Shannah satyasya suyamasyashansah shanno aryama purujatoastu.

(May our riches bring us happiness and may our praise be conducive to our peace. May our sharp intellect work to enhance our happiness and may our wealth increase our peace. May disciplined, truthful speech enhance our happiness. O Supreme Judge of Judges, may your justice spread happiness and peace.)

—RIG VEDA 7.35.2

Wealth is necessary for survival and a reasonable amount of wealth is necessary for a decent living. A man who is steeped in poverty and does not have enough wealth to satisfy his bare needs can hardly be at peace with himself and his surroundings. The hymns of the Vedas refer to wealth and prosperity at multiple places and exhort humankind to exert itself and persevere to earn wealth. Poverty is the greatest curse that can befall a person. But when the Vedas refer to the term 'aishwarya' (prosperity) as something that everyone should strive for, what do they convey? How much wealth should a person accumulate? Wealth is earned through collective and collaborative effort called yagya. Wealth should be earned through rightful and legitimate means so that benefits accrue to all equitably. Disparity and disproportionate distribution of wealth is abnormal and unnatural and disruptive of peace.

Wealth for fulfilment of needs brings peace; wealth for fulfilment of greed disrupts peace. Hence, the amount of wealth should be only as much as is commensurate with your genuine needs, which also include the need to serve others and promote their material welfare. The latter justifies the creation of more wealth through collaborative economic activities such as trade and business.

Speech as an instrument of human welfare refers to the positive characteristics pertaining to speech—courtesy, truthfulness, politeness and humility. These characteristics make speech productive and useful and conducive to peace and harmony. Courtesy and politeness in speech create an aura of positivity. Humility in speech helps to strengthen the bonds of love and respect between interacting humans. Foul speech damages respect and relationship. The quality of speech is so very important that it virtually rules human relationships and determines the outcome of human endeavour in many areas involving verbal interaction. With humility, one can overpower one's rank enemy and through arrogant and uncouth speech estrange one's closest of friends.

> *Speak when you are angry and you'll make the best speech you'll ever regret.*
>
> —LAURENCE J. PETER

Anger and angry state are the antitheses of peace. Beneficial speech is delivered only in a peaceful state of mind and conversely only beneficial speech establishes peace. Both complement each other. Uncouth or irritated speech is the outcome of a mind that is ill at ease. Speech laced with irritation creates more problems than it solves. It should be understood that anger is the root cause of most of the problems pertaining to interpersonal relationships. Anger vitiates the intellect and for the period it occupies the mental space, it destroys a person's capability to think and act logically. Any words spoken in an angry state invariably turn out to be self-damaging and destroying.

What is the meaning of intellect as an instrument of human welfare?

Intellect is the prime vehicle for all human actions. It is the intellect that holds the mind and bridles it. The mind on its own runs helter-skelter. It is so erratic and excitable that left to itself, it can take its owner into the cesspool of misery, into a bottomless pit and into the mouth of hell, while pursuing pleasure, enjoyment and gratification. Hedonism is a prime characteristic of the frail mind. But the mind does not have an isolated existence. It is controlled by the intellect. It is only when this control is loosened that troubles begin to surface. Intellect, its refinement and application, has been considered so important that it forms a part of the 10 cardinal principles of dharma (righteousness). Therefore, intellect is the most important entity in a human being and constitutes the prime vehicle for one's progress.

> *The voice of the intellect is a soft one, but it does not rest until it has gained a hearing.*
>
> —SIGMUND FREUD

Man is driven by intellect. When the intellect is benumbed or confused, we wallow in illusion. Our development is stalled or retarded. The intellect may know what is right and what is wrong, but if its hold on the erratic mind is weak, the result is frequently the same—retardation of human progress. Ultimately, through inner curiosity and its gradual satisfaction, we understand the core truths of life and become aligned with them. That alignment is progress, in real terms. That alignment is spiritual transcendence.

Judgments play a crucial role too in the establishment and maintenance of human peace. When does a person fail to make right judgments? When does one ignore the principles of equity and fairness? One may do this for two reasons. The first is one's inability or failure to understand the truth. The other is deliberate disregard of truth. The latter may occur because of selfish instincts. Erratic judgment results in erratic action and the inevitable result is the disruption of peace and harmony. The higher a person is placed in the social hierarchy in formal or informal institutions, the more is the importance of his/her judgments. Especially this is so in the case of judges and administrators. The judgments of the governing elite are crucial to the interests of a large number of people, as these judgments have a wide repercussion. To deliver good judgments, one has to be unbiased and also compassionate towards the wronged party.

Make no judgments where you have no compassion.
—ANNE MCCAFFREY

Judgments delivered by a person in position of command, responsibility or power need to be fair and equitable. But such judgments can be arrived at only if that person has internal peace. If there is internal peace, there is bound to be a sense of fairness and empathy towards others. There is bound to be compassion. The very presence of compassion in a person means that one is mentally postured to lend a helping hand, to help alleviate others' miseries and problems. Compassion is a divine quality. It is attributed to the creator

God. Hence, it is a godly trait. Compassion in a person does not mean that one is inclined to extend out of turn favours to others. That would be violation of natural justice. It means that the people who have been wronged, exploited or oppressed should be helped. It also means that people who have been naturally less endowed should be helped to come up. It means uplifting of the underprivileged.

The understanding of and attitude towards wealth are important to make it an instrument of happiness. You have to look at the haves and have-nots. People struck by poverty and deprivation need wealth. Look at the people living in stark poverty in subhuman conditions, dwelling in shanty hutments and barely eking out an existence. Even today, more than three billion people in the world live on less than USD2.5 a day. They should be helped. People with overflowing wealth do not need that much wealth. They should not hoard it. They should rather put their wealth to good use by offering it to the needy either through charity or through investment in productive projects, which in turn will create jobs and reduce poverty. Wealth when hoarded becomes liable for destruction. It has to keep flowing; it needs to be continually used for the benefit of others.

But what do we observe today? We find wealth siphoned out of countries and kept in faraway lands. We have so many tax havens in today's world, where illegitimate wealth is stashed away. At many places, it is simply hoarded and not used in any manner. Such wealth hoarders have to pay hefty charges to agencies who keep their wealth secure. Whether it is Swiss banks or agencies in Mauritius, Saint Kitts and Nevis, and Bermuda, the story is the same everywhere. Such wealth, most of which is generated by wrongful means, is a cause of misery to millions. Huge amounts of illegitimate money flows across borders of countries by way of money laundering and humungous amounts come back to the corrupt money originators through 'round tripping operations'. This is what we ought not to do with money. This is what perpetuates poverty on the globe. This is what has been deplored by the Vedas.

Let me reiterate that speech has to be polite and truthful to promote inner wellness. Relationships hinge on what we speak, how we speak and when we speak. Relationships crumbling today are a silent testimony to indiscreet speech. Speech laced with anger and arrogance damages relationships between husband and wife. It creates distance between peers at work. It creates mistrust between a consultant and his/her client. It erodes faith between a physician and his/her patient. It undermines trust in fiduciary relationships.

You only have to deliberately work upon the tone and tenor of your speech, otherwise benign in content, to see the wonders it works in your relationships. The problems from the nagging spouse, from the bullying peer, from the complaining boss are really the problems with the tone and tenor of speech. If only they controlled this aspect of their speech, it would not disrupt inner peace and harmony. But, as stated above, you need to speak the truth too. And truth is often bitter. What if the boss needs to tell his/her subordinate that he/she is slipshod in his/her work or the wife needs to tell her husband of his unseemly habits? They should convey the truths politely and humbly so that the truth doesn't hurt, yet the message is effectively conveyed.

Intellect is the most underutilized faculty today. People act impulsively, without applying their sense of logic and suffer the baneful consequences. People have a puffed-up ego that doesn't allow them to understand issues in the right perspective. Applying your innate sense of logic to situations is also an art that needs to be learnt and developed. When the conservative father doesn't understand the perspective of his modern liberal son, he tends to behave in an over doting or over dominating or over interfering manner. And that spoils the relationship between father and son. When the son fails to understand his father's perspective, he regards his parent selfish, inward-looking and narrow-minded even though that perception be untrue. Similarly, the constantly complaining mother-in-law fails to understand the perspective of her daughter-in-law. And the dissatisfied employee at workplace who is denied promotion fails to understand the real reason why his/her employer acted the way he/she did—to do justice to other employees and the larger organization. Proper application of the intellect on the part of individuals would prevent this.

Judgments, whether in the mind or expressly stated, have a lot to do with the quality of our relationships. After all, your attitude and behaviour directly depend on what sort of judgment you hold about people or situations. Judgments also have a lot to do with the preservation of fairness and equity in the world.

> *Do not condemn the judgment of another because it differs from your own. You may both be wrong.*
>
> —DANDEMIS

Judgments announced by legal functionaries of the government in courts need to be fair and they should uphold the tenets of justice. God is just. He dispenses perfect justice to His human subjects because He is omniscient and omnipotent. But human beings are not all knowing. They have to base their judgments on pieces of evidence gathered from various sources. In many cases, imperfect, incoherent or inaccurate information is gathered that adversely affects the process of judgment. They have to base their judgments on the laws of the land which may not be perfect and equitable in all cases. But above all, they have to be honest and impartial in dispensing justice. We are privy to the guilty being buried of his charges and the innocent being convicted. We are also witness to judgments of district courts being upturned by high courts and the judgments of high courts upturned by the Supreme Court. This tells the story of dispensation of imperfect justice. Sound judgments with the element of compassion in them hold the key to preservation of equity and fairness in the human society. They are important for peace and harmony—inner or outer.

This mantra of the Vedas emphasizes the need for exercising prudence in judging individuals and situations in our lives. We ought to remain unbiased and free from the hold of passion while making or passing judgments. If we erred in this, wrong judgments and unjust actions on that basis will continue to haunt us in our subconscious minds and torment us internally. Our inner peace will remain disrupted. Wrong judgments pronounced on individuals would also do the same—disrupt harmony and peace among them.

The effect of continuous incantation of this divine mantra is that it refines one's intellect and waters down his pride and arrogance. It also works to diminish one's passion and make him/her level-headed. It makes one's speech polite and helps in betterment of relationships. All this happens through tapping of that infinite pool of positivity and beneficence in which the individual human soul is fully immersed. When our mind and intellect are positively affected through divine intervention, it spells peace and happiness for us.

THREE

Incantations for Happiness and Well-Being

Aum shannodhata shamudharta no astu shannah uruchi bhavatu swadhabhi. Sham rodasi brihati shanno adri shanno devanaam suhavani santu.

(May the Lord who is our nourisher and supporter bestow peace on us. May this earth with its various resources promote our welfare. May this earth and the light-filled ether promote our peace. May the clouds and mountains enhance our happiness! May the prayers of the learned and erudite be full of peace.)

—RIG VEDA 7.35.3

Peace from all quarters connotes the vibrations of harmony from all sides. Vibrations of harmony are really the messages and stimuli that are likeable, favourable and tolerable. Some of these messages or notes may be directly of your preference and taste. They would at once be likeable. Other notes may not be in accordance with your taste and you may find them disturbing, irritating or even abhorrent. When we analyse the meaning of peace from all quarters, we have to relook at its composite definition. The word 'peace' means calmness, harmony and purity. Excessive noise disturbs calmness and is antithetical to peace. Harmony is what has been described in the above lines. Purity is the homogeneity of the natural elements around us—the elements called water, air, foodgrains, fruits, vegetables and medicinal herbs. The hymn of the Veda under explanation prays to the Almighty for peace from all the six spatial directions—east, west, north, south, top and bottom. Our peace and inner well-being depend upon the qualitative and quantitative flow of natural elements towards us and the kind of vibes we receive from others, including other living beings. But, at the same time, the way in which we receive these external stimuli also determines our inner peace.

> *Even a fool, when he holdeth his peace, is counted wise.*
> —PROVERB 17:28, BIBLICAL PROVERB

God will bestow peace on us based on our karma, which means based on how we handle His creation consisting of Mother Nature and other sentient beings. God is 100 per cent just in His actions. Therefore, to expect that in response to our prayers, He will set in motion a chain of events that will establish peace in spite of our unrighteous karma is too far-fetched and unrealistic. Yes, we can pray to the Almighty for peace, which means we will seek to tap His infinite energy for refining our character and actions. That refinement will inexorably bring us peace. Therefore, we are indirectly seeking peace from the Creator through our prayers. Purity is the watchword here. It is purity of our actions performed through thoughts in the mind, speech and working of our senses that will bring us peace.

> *Purity is right. Impurity is wrong. True? Absolutely. But it's equally correct to say purity is always smart; impurity is always stupid. There it is—what I'm calling The Purity*

Principle: Purity is always smart; impurity is always stupid. Not sometimes. Not usually. Always. You're not an exception. I'm not an exception. There are no exceptions. A holy God made the universe in such a way that actions true to His character, and the laws derived from His character, are always rewarded. Actions that violate His character, however, are always punished. He rewards every act of justice; He punishes every act of injustice.
—RANDY ALCORN, *The Purity Principle*

Purity is the crux of godliness and spirituality. Hence, it is the basis of peace and harmony in the world. When purity is compromised with, peace suffers a sure casualty. The earth with its abundant resources has been created to enable the highest-grade sentient beings—humans—to liberate themselves. The natural resources—air, water, cereals, fruits, vegetables, etc.—nourish our bodies, minds and intellects. This nourishment would be undermined by impurities in these resources. Human welfare lies in living in sync with nature and following the prime tenets of dharma. Therefore, the basis of human welfare is inner and outer peace and, as stated above, the basis of peace in turn is purity.

The entire space we see around us, seemingly with infinite expanse in all directions, is ether. Light from the luminous celestial objects such as the sun and the moon fills the ethereal space. The ether, being one of the five cardinal elements of nature, is a part of our body, mind, intellect and ego. Hence, if we allow the impurities of material nature to pervade our body, mind, intellect or ego, the ether, which is a constituent of these four entities, will not remain undefiled. Then it will neither promote our peace, nor enhance progress.

The Vedic mantra then talks of clouds and mountains

enhancing our happiness level. Clouds that bring timely and adequate rainfall for our agricultural fields and other vegetation will maintain the production of cereals, fruits and vegetables for our healthy sustenance. The grassy lands and lush forests maintained so by regular rainfall will ensure fodder for our milk-producing cattle. But clouds pouring out excessive rain will also flood our mainland and countryside. Therefore, rainfall has to be of controlled intensity to be conducive to human health and happiness.

Finally, the hymn refers to the prayers of learned scholars which, to be effective and fruitful, should be fully aligned with nature and entirely selfless. Prayers to the Almighty for fulfilment of narrow human desires have always been in evidence. But prayers by the learned for specific desires should be directed at mass welfare and altruistic to bring best beneficial results.

Prayers to the Almighty, the Creator and the Sustainer have to be for the good of all, occasioned by fairness and justice to all. In this perspective, prayers can never be pure if they are merely for the fulfilment of narrow desires. In the operation of this large universe where all events happen due to past actions and connections, these events cannot but be the harbingers of seamless divine justice to one and all.

This hymn of the Rig Veda talks of Mother Earth and her resources, as explained above. As further explained, the purity of these resources matters a lot. The lower animals live their lives in fully natural ways. They do not possess the high grade of intellect that humans are endowed with. In order that this high grade of intellect may help the cause of general peace and well-being of all inhabitants on this planet, the Creator gave us knowledge in the form of the Vedas. It is in proper application of this knowledge that human peace, prosperity and deliverance lie.

We humans have polluted not only the air and the water around us but also the pure knowledge handed down to us by the Creator. In fact, pollution of knowledge in the form of its distortion or corruption is the fundamental factor in pollution of other things. Because of distortion of true knowledge, our ideologies are corrupted. Instead of one religion of all humanity—the fundamental Vedic religion, there are in evidence hundreds and thousands of religions, sects and cults. Many of them are partially distorted versions of the original Vedic dharma.

Today, you do not see the mainstream religions of the world—Christianity, Islam, Hinduism, Zoroastrianism, Buddhism—concurring on ideological tenets. Within one religion like Islam, you observe the sects Shias and Sunnis constantly at loggerheads. Hundreds of sub-sects and hundreds of cults show various shades of the same ideology. They seem to have starkly different ways of looking at the same thing, different solutions to the same problem and sometimes widely differing approaches to doing the same thing. To the extent that these differences do not cause friction between communities, it is all right. But when these differences begin to create conflicts, problems arise. Therefore, uniformity and unanimity of thought are needed for the establishment of durable harmony and peace. And this can be achieved only by dissemination of true knowledge that will dispel ignorance and remove misunderstandings.

Dialogue and discussion should take the place of compartmentalized thinking. People should discuss and iron out their sharply differing ideas and perceptions. In the present world of emails and WhatsApp, there is excellent connectivity but not extensive dialogue. Many people seem to be dwelling within the cellars of their minds and are unreceptive to different lines of thinking. This is not conducive to harmony. This does not promote peace.

We are witness to parent-offspring relationships cracking because of the absence of dialogue. In a large house where parents and grown-up children occupy separate rooms at different floors, the parents and children often communicate through SMS and WhatsApp messages. There appear to be walls between their minds thicker than the concrete walls separating their rooms. Similar situations appear to exist in sibling relationships, conjugal relationships and professional-peer relationships. Relationships are breaking under the load of mutual expectations. This is an unseemly situation. Enlightened dialogue is the answer to these issues.

The one element of behaviour that prevents reconciliatory dialogue is anger. The other such element is pride. All scriptures of the world are unanimous on anger and arrogance as the cardinal evils of human behaviour and unequivocally denounce them. Because of these evils pervading our minds, compassion does not develop. Absence of compassion does not allow cooperation and conciliation. It makes people selfish and egocentric. What is required is an approach that will make people more selfless.

Today, a large proportion of the learned people and scholars seems to be working entirely for itself or for self-aggrandizement. Their pure knowledge needs to be backed by pure intentions. Their prayers to the Creator should have that element of altruism to be effective and fruitful.

What does the practice of this mantra connote for an ordinary individual? Like every other mantra of the Vedas, incantation of this mantra by a person connects him with his Creator, God. The earth, the ether, the clouds and the mountains will bring us peace and happiness only if we follow the scientific laws of nature and protect it from degradation. The effect of incantation of this mantra will serve to guide the intellect and mind of the person in the right direction for right action that will preserve the purity of nature. It will make the literates and the educated more learned and compassionate. It will bring people more in tune with nature and the eternal, inviolable laws of nature.

FOUR

Peace Promotion through Preceptors and Individual Conduct

Om shanno agnirjyotiraniko astu shanno mitra varunavashvinashamah. Shannah sukritaam sukritani santu shannah ishiro abhi vatu vatah.

(O Lord Agni, Mitra, Varun and the teacher and preceptor Ashwini Deva! Bestow peace upon us. May the deeds performed by noble souls enhance our happiness. May the flow of this vital element—air—bring us happiness and peace.)

—RIG VEDA 3.35.4

This hymn of the Rig Veda talks of the terms 'Agni', 'Mitra', 'Varun' and 'Ashwini' as the names of almighty God. Each name stands for a special attribute. Agni means that who is the embodiment of knowledge, is omniscient, worthy of knowing and attaining and also worthy of worship. Mitra connotes that who loves all. Varun is that who, being noblest, possesses superlative positive qualities. Ashwini means powerful and complete. The incantation to the Almighty in this hymn is for attaining true knowledge, which forms the vehicle of human progress and is the foundation of righteous deeds that eventually lead to peace and happiness.

Peace and happiness are the inevitable products of

right conduct and action. Any human action that promotes the welfare of other living beings including other humans is right action. This action is conducive to protection of the environment, preservation of ecological balance and the natural pattern of the ecosphere with its 8.4 million species of flora and fauna. It also means preservation of the wholesomeness of physical environment.

> *Happiness is like a butterfly; the more you chase it, the more it will elude you, but if you turn your attention to other things, it will come and sit softly on your shoulder.*
> —HENRY DAVID THOREAU

Right conduct and action is dharma. The entire universe including the earth and its inhabitants is ruled by dharma and dharma is defined by the undermentioned 10 cardinal abiding principles.

1. Patience
2. Forgiveness
3. Truthfulness
4. True knowledge
5. Cleanliness of body and mind
6. Control of the senses
7. Mind control
8. Honesty
9. Intellectual application
10. Abjuring anger

To enhance inner peace and happiness, we need to understand and be aware at all times that human life is neither a bed of roses nor a bed of thorns. It is both. Adversities and obstacles that stifle our happiness are part and parcel of life. We must learn to deal with them with firmness and fortitude. Once we do it, other issues will take care of themselves and fall in place.

It's part of life to have obstacles. It's about overcoming obstacles; that's the key to happiness.
—HERBIE HANCOCK

Knowledge of dharma is the foundation of peace and happiness. Knowledge of dharma connotes a true practical understanding of the above tenets. This practical understanding is built upon experience and not rote learning. It is built upon a series of incidents or episodes which are in the nature of retributive effects of human karmas. Knowledge is much more than information. In fact, it is more than information and understanding combined. It is information and true understanding of things. It is the antithesis of ignorance and illusion. It is the prime attribute of the human soul. It is the vehicle for human peace, prosperity and progress. God referred to as Agni is all knowledgeable. It is the most worthwhile thing for humans to understand Him and worship Him. Knowledge flows like a stream of nectar from the omniscient Almighty to His ardent worshipper.

The omnipresent divine entity who is all powerful and loves all is always in the friendly and compassionate mode. Worship of that entity brings serenity and peace in unmistakable terms. It brings harmony in relationships. It brings purity of thought and calmness in the mind.

The other attribute of almighty God is the supreme nobility because of which we can always expect goodness and nothing but goodness from Him. This goodness may also be veiled as punishment for our misdeeds but, all the same, it is for the overall good of everyone and based on perfect justice.

We humans are incomplete in knowledge and understanding and our Creator is complete, being all knowing. Therefore, it makes perfect sense to connect with Him through worship for refinement of mind and intellect and thereby for acquisition of true knowledge. As mentioned above, true knowledge also directly flows from the realm of the Almighty to His human subject during meditative communion with Him.

What has the primordial physical element of air to do with the subject of human peace and happiness? A huge lot.

Air element is the medium through which human senses operate. It flows through the physical channels called nerves in the human body and all the five physical senses of touch, taste, smell, hearing and sight function through it. The moment there is any imbalance in this vital element, perception is adversely affected. The mind and intellect are affected too. Consequently, the quality of our karmas is affected. Improper or inappropriate karmas attract adverse retributive effects according to the inviolable law of cause and effect. The result is erosion of peace and happiness.

In the context of this hymn of the Rig Veda, the role of the earthly knowledge giver or preceptor is emphasized. The preceptor or guru is the person who passes on that knowledge to us and dispels the darkness of our minds. True knowledge being the foundation of peace, the guru or guide becomes the instrument of attainment of that peace. While a scripture is an inanimate instrument of bringing knowledge, the guru is the live instrument and hence, more important.

In today's world, perhaps the most misunderstood and misinterpreted term is 'religion'. Often, the English term 'religion' is equated with the Hindi and Sanskrit term 'dharma'. This is outright incorrect. In common usage, the two terms are used in the same context, which has created wide misgivings as to the actual meaning and nature of dharma. Dharma is equated with sects or cults. There are many of them in today's world—Christianity, Islam, Hinduism, Zoroastrianism, Buddhism, Sikhism and their variants and shades. They bear different brands and labels. We ought to understand the true meaning of dharma and of religion which connotes the religion of humanity. The religion of humanity is that code of conduct which needs to be adopted by every human being and which has been spelt out in the previous page. It is that code which, if followed, maintains peace, progress and prosperity. Dharma is actually righteousness, and not religion.

Is today's teacher or preceptor equipped with the right knowledge to enhance peace and happiness? Is he/she aligned with the principles of universal dharma as referred above in His working? Is he/she dedicated to the cause of truth and true knowledge? Is his/her concern limited to information enhancement of his/her pupils or he/she goes beyond that—to knowledge refinement and character improvement? The answers to all these questions are amply clear. Today's teachers, whether at the kindergarten stage or high-school level or at the university level are functioning more like mercenaries than like the dispellers of darkness in the sense conveyed by this Vedic hymn. We need to review and reform our teachers' roles as well as the course contents of our educational institutions. We need to make education holistic. We desperately require an overhaul of the systems of education to transform academic courses from narrow vocational grooming plans to knowledge-, skills- and character-building plans.

Air element is vital to all sentient beings. Air is the basis of terrestrial life. But today, this very basic vital element stands heavily degraded and polluted. The carbon dioxide content in the earth's atmosphere, which has been stable at 0.02 per cent for ages, has gradually increased to 0.03 per cent in the last 100 years—thanks to the millions of octane-guzzling automobiles running on the roads and airplanes in thousands flying across the skies. This is not to mention the huge number of pollutant gas-emitting factories all over the globe.

The flow of the vital element called air will bring peace to humans only when this element is pure and purged of pollutants.

> *Water and air, the two essential fluids on which all life depends, have become global garbage cans.*
> —JACQUES-YVES COUSTEAU

Mitigation of air pollution is a big challenge today. We perhaps need a thorough change of technologies in our manufacturing industry and aviation industry or even a paradigm shift in our living priorities to forestall the calamitous conditions that air pollution and its fallout—climate change—seem to be bringing.

What is the solution then?

We need to look into the superior, environment-friendly technologies delineated in the Vedas. Let us not forget that this earth is more than 1.96 billion years old and humanity has been in existence for nearly that much period. The eternal knowledge of the Vedas was passed on to the earliest of humans. Generations of humans have lived here and have learned and applied this Vedic knowledge. They have learnt and unlearnt things, riding the crest and trough of a civilized existence. Definitely, superior technologies were used by the earlier generations and need to be revived today—for sheer survival.

At the individual level, regular performing of the *agnihotra yagya* (sacrificial fire ritual) prescribed in the Yajur Veda is the way to mitigate atmospheric pollution. This ritual is the single most potent means to combat the heavy air pollution existing today. It works subtly and scientifically. The fumes emanating from the sacrificial fire fuelled by select natural substances purify the air in the ratio of 1:1 million by volume. They help to restore the balance of the gaseous constituents of the atmosphere besides killing pathogenic bacteria and viruses. The technology behind *agnihotra yagya* comes from the master of the universe and all creation and has to be perfect, even if it is presently beyond the comprehension of human mortals. Beyond doubt, it purifies even the other four panchabhut elements—water, fire, earth and ether. The outbreak of pandemic caused by Coronavirus in December 2019 and its global spread in the subsequent months created a calamitous situation. Mass-scale performance of *agnihotra yagya* could be an effective means to control the pandemic.

Apart from what has been stated above, this mantra of the Vedas exhorts human beings to understand true dharma and indoctrinate their future generations on that basis. The principles or tenets of true dharma have been listed earlier in this chapter. These form the foundation of peace and progress and whatever comes in conflict with these tenets has to be understood as an impediment to this peace and progress. Daily efforts in alignment with the basic tenets of dharma continuously polishes a person, making him more humane. After all, humanism is true religion that provides a person the plan for peace and prosperity.

FIVE

Flow and Intensity of Nature's Elements

*Aum shanno dyavaprithivi purvahutaou
shamantariksham drishaye no astu. Shannah
aushadhirvanino bhavantu shanno rajasaspatirastu
jishnu.*

(May the electricity and earth elements, extolled by our ancestors, bring peace to us. May the ethereal space give us peace, bringing a wealth of knowledge to us. May the herbs and trees enhance our peace. May the hub of all planetary bodies—the sun—bring us peace.)

—RIG VEDA 7.35.5

Electricity is a form or variant of Agni, one of the five primordial material elements. The earth is another of those five elements. Electricity and earth elements have a crucial role to play in our happiness, peace and prosperity. Our ancestors—the erudite sages and savants—have studied the properties of electricity and earth comprehensively and had written volumes in their potential for enhancing human prosperity. There are many mantras in the Vedas that talk of electricity and the multifarious ways in which its potential can be exploited for enhancing human prosperity.

The modern world shows the marvels of electricity in full glow. Electricity is an essential element of our daily life. We cannot survive without it. It has the potential to beneficially touch every sphere of our life. It finds application in every walk of life, from birth till death. Every institution and every human activity makes use of electricity in some form or the other. Whether it is fluorescent lights, electric fans, air conditioners, telephones, the internet, wireless telephones or mobile phones, it is indispensable in our daily life. Our factories producing various types of consumer and industrial goods run on electricity. All means of transport—cars, trains, ships and airplanes—use electricity in various ways, either to generate motive power or to run ignition system or for the functioning of instrumentation and control systems. Electricity is the core functional element in warfare equipment. Modern artillery, fighter aircrafts, missile systems and nuclear armaments—all use electricity in some way or another. It finds application in the production and delivery of every manufactured product that comes to us. It is the biggest boon of modern science. And its applications for increasing human comfort and convenience are on the rise.

Our ancestors were indeed men of knowledge and wisdom to have talked of electricity back then.

The earth element belongs to the solid earth, which is our celestial abode. You can go on counting for hours the various types of metals, minerals, herbs, plants, trees, fruits and vegetables that the earth provides for our sustenance and fulfilment. And there are multiple ways in which these substances benefit us and increase our level of comfort, happiness, satisfaction and fulfilment. Indeed, the creator God has bestowed on us many, many bounties.

But the moot question that arises in the context of this mantra is: how will electricity and earth element enhance our peace?

Yes, the important point to note in this connection is that both these substances need to be used judiciously. We ought to know how to produce, handle and apply them in our daily lives without any kind of collateral harm. The conventional modes of producing electricity during the past 150 years—thermal power generation, hydro power generation and nuclear power generation—have, of late, been found to be environment unfriendly. We are now shifting to renewable sources of power such as solar and wind power in a big way. We must protect the physical environment and the ecosphere. We have to maintain our physical and mental health. We must know how to dispose of the wastes generated in our manufacturing plants which use substances extracted from Mother Earth. We should be able to recycle non-biodegradable wastes. Or we should be able to produce things on a mass scale without generating non-biodegradable waste residues. We should be aware of the techniques and technologies that do not inflict damage on the environment. We must not use electricity for producing nuclear arsenal and other weapons of mass destruction. Electricity is power and power must be used prudently and for the betterment of mankind.

Power which can be abused, will be abused.
—JIM WARNER

We ought to use electricity (or electrical power) carefully and cautiously. The indiscriminate use of X-rays for medical diagnostic purposes has brought collateral harm. The widespread use of mobile telephony is attended by the construction of microwave-emitting towers all over and this has filled a large space with microwave radiation, which is suspected to be harmful for our health and more so for birds and lower animals. Many species of birds including the ubiquitous sparrow have changed their habitation patterns because of the concentration of mobile telephony towers in certain regions.

Trees and herbs will enhance human health and happiness only when they are nourished by pure soil, water and air. If we play havoc with the purity of water, air as well as soil, the herbs, vegetables, fruits and the vegetation, in general, will be impure too and not conducive to our health and well-being. This is the lesson that modern man needs to urgently learn.

> *People who will not sustain trees will soon live in a world that will not sustain people.*
>
> —BRYCE NELSON

We badly need to preserve the purity and wholesomeness of the vital elements that trees, shrubs and herbs absorb to sustain themselves and, in turn, to sustain humans and other animals on this planet.

The lord of the planetary system—the sun—is the source of all energy for terrestrial beings. That energy has to come in controlled intensity to be beneficial for these beings including humans. The earth's atmospheric layers including the ozone layer absorb much of the ionizing, harmful radiation that forms part of the sun's rays. When filtered through the stratosphere, mesosphere and ionosphere including the ozone layer, the solar radiation becomes beneficial for human beings and that is what has been sought through the incantation of this mantra. This will happen when we keep the atmosphere in pure form—maintaining the natural proportion of oxygen, nitrogen, carbon dioxide, water vapour and other gaseous constituents. We need to run all our factories and industrial units as also transportation vehicles in an environment-friendly manner.

This mantra carries beneficial effects through chanting even at the individual level. The positive and healthy vibrations produced by its chanting serve to regulate and normalize the body heat existing in the form of pitta and thereby prevent the occurrence of diseases such as sunstroke, bilious ailments, hyperacidity (gastritis), angina (coronary artery disease), ulcers and quinsy (inflammation of the throat). Regular chanting of this mantra pacifies the excessive pitta in the human body and helps to prevent or cure these diseases.

The average individual can get the message of using environment-friendly techniques and technologies in his daily life from this mantra. He can choose to use jute and paper bags instead of plastic ones; he can wear cotton garments instead of nylon- or polyester-based ones; he can store potable water in copper or steel vessels rather than in plastic containers; he can use electric automobiles instead of the diesel- or petrol-guzzling ones. The underlying thought and conviction are that core scientific truths need not be discovered by man; they are all available eternally in the Vedas—the scriptures sourced to the omniscient God. We have to create products out of material nature and use them in accordance with the principles expounded in the Vedas and other texts derived from them. Only then can we sustain and survive.

Nature-compatible and environment-friendly techniques will thus have to be developed and embraced.

SIX

Indra, Varun and Rudra: The Harbingers of Peace

Aum shannah indro vasubhirdevo shanno astu shamadityebhirvaruna sushansah. Shanno rudro rudrebhirjalashah shannahstvashta grabhiriha shrinotu.

(May the bestower of wealth and material bounties Indra Dev bring us happiness. May the water dispersed in the ethereal space enhance our well-being. Lord Rudra, the embodiment of peace who punishes the wicked, may bring happiness to us. The learned folks, through their auspicious speech, may give us sermons of peace and bless us.)

—RIG VEDA 7.35.6, ATHARVA VEDA 19.10.6

The phrase 'peace and happiness from wealth' carries the connotations of a truly great message. Such a message could flow only from a divine source of knowledge like the Vedas. This message conveys that wealth and other material bounties can bring us happiness only if they are created through righteous means and are also used properly. The term 'dharma' is inextricably attached to human peace and happiness.

The use of the term 'dharma' takes us back to Chapter 4, where its definition was provided in detail. Dharma is the set of human dos and don'ts that promote universal welfare. It may be noted in this context that one of the 10-point human code of action and conduct called dharma includes true knowledge. This true knowledge tells us how to create wealth and spend it. It also tells us how *not* to create wealth and how *not* to use it. True knowledge is the knowledge provided in the Vedas. Every thread of knowledge applied in wealth creation and distribution needs to be consistent with Vedic ideology for it to be conducive to human happiness. Let us, therefore, eschew corrupt means of generating wealth.

The person who doesn't know where his next dollar is coming from usually doesn't know where his last dollar went.

—UNKNOWN

Let us, therefore, be very particular about our means of earning or creating wealth and the sources of that wealth. Any questionable means of generating money will disrupt peace and harmony, both outside and inside of us. It will undermine our inner wellness.

The Vedic hymn under exposition talks of Indra—the material god of wealth, Varun—the god of water and Rudra—the god of peace. Accordingly, the subject of water comes next in the discussion.

Water is the most fundamental element for human sustenance. In fact, about 70 per cent of the human body is made up of water. But we have to be careful and discreet in our usage of water. The quantity and quality of water that we consume has a direct bearing on our general health, both physical and mental. How we handle and manage water resources on our planet affects the quality of our environment and indirectly that of our lives.

That brings us to the last point concerning the learned folks and the sermons of peace from them. These learned folks are the erudite people who have studied the Vedas and have moulded their lives in accordance with the injunctions of the Vedas. The hymn is an incantation to the creator God seeking peace through sermons and blessings from the learned people. We now turn our attention to the current scenario in regard to the various points touched upon by this hymn.

Let us look at the way wealth is being created and used in the world today. Capitalism still rules the roost. Even in the historically communist countries like China, the trend of recent decades has been towards creation of huge factories to feed the entire world. The Western countries including America and west Europe have been the harbingers of capitalism as seen from their models of economic growth since the eighteenth century. Following the flow of fulsome wealth caused by economic plunder and depredations of the colonized countries, Britain, Spain and France underwent huge industrial revolutions. These revolutions spread to other countries of the European continent. Big manufacturing plants and factories emerged over a period of time and multinational corporations (MNCs) began to dominate global business and money growth. But was this scheme of wealth creation truly in line with the divine injunctions of the Vedas?

Money spent on narcotics/drugs, intoxicant liquor and tobacco products, which are harmful for our health and not conducive to happiness and peace, is not money well spent. Money spent on bribery, smuggling, espionage, terrorist and secessionist activities and other similar illegal activities will also destroy peace, beyond doubt.

The above are examples to illustrate how money should

not be earned and spent.

Water is a prime life element in nature. This primal element for human living needs to be kept pure and free of pollution for it to remain beneficial for human consumption and also consumption by the lower animals, trees and plants. The deleterious effects of impure water on the human body tell a sordid tale of its degradation, disease and decay. Today, water pollution caused by industrial effluents has assumed alarming proportions. It is taking a heavy toll on aquatic life and telling upon the health of a wide variety of flora and fauna existing on land. Modern medical science claims to know a lot about the human body's functioning but to understand the right quantity, right quality, proper mode of intake and right time of intake of water, we need to borrow from the ancient wisdom of Ayurveda. Water, according to Atharva Veda, is one of the best medicines.

If there is magic force on this planet, it is contained in water.

—LOREN EISELEY

We need to adopt water-management and water-consumption practices in line with the principles prescribed in the Vedas and other texts derived from them. That will prevent water pollution and maintain balance of water distribution on the planet. Water-consumption habits in line with the divine science of Ayurveda will help us to use water for maintenance of optimal health.

Now we take the subject of 'learned folks'. The Vedas talk of learned folks at several places. They are the ones who have grasped and assimilated the message of Vedic hymns and are living their lives in line with those messages. They are the ones who can teach us the theory and practice of

Vedic injunctions and can be the instruments of our spiritual growth. They are the ones who need to be revered. We should invite them to our homes and listen to their sermons.

Let the sermons of the erudite scholars enhance our peace and happiness. This is going to be possible if we give respect to the learned people. But what is happening today? Many of the truly learned ones are living in obscurity and neglect. The semi-learned ones who have also learned the art of marketing are grabbing all the attention and many of them have made flourishing business out of lecturing.

The practice of disseminating the higher truths has been commercialized too!

We are living in an age of mercenaries and money-mongers. Money has become the central theme of our lives. Politics and religion too have become money-centric. This is unfortunate and we need to change it. Knowledge is powerful and more valuable than money, not the other way round. The Vedic hymn under reference brings home this sublime message. In this age of falsities and deception, we need to beware of fake preachers and sermonizers. There are plenty of them around and many have a huge fan following too. Many such god-men have been implicated in heinous crimes such as rape and murder. Let there be genuine scholars to guide us to a peaceful and happy living. Incantation of such prayer will invoke the blessings of the Almighty to make it happen.

In many societies, some people, out of strong religious faith, tend to become very naïve and impressionable. They are easily swayed by deceptive god-men and sermonizers. There are well-known instances of some womenfolk falling easy prey to the antics of fake god-men. We have to steer clear of them. It is important to get above superstitions and grow a scientific temper. Development of scientific temper, in accordance with the message of this Vedic hymn, will produce rational-minded preachers and rational-minded followers among us, thus paving the way for peace, progress and prosperity.

SEVEN

Peace Enhancement through Elements of Yagya

Aum shannah somobhavatu brahma shannah shanno gravanah shamusantuyagyaa. Shannah swarunaam mitayo bhavantu shannah prasvah shamvastuvedi.

(May all herbs and foodgrains enhance our peace and happiness. May all the human contrivances of comfort bring us peace. All types of yagya should enhance human peace. May this place for performance of yagya be peace promoting. May all herbs and plants promote our health and longevity. May the havan kunda enhance our peace.)
—RIG VEDA 7.35.7; YAJUR VEDA 15.22;
ATHARVA VEDA 19.10.7

How will or will not the herbs, cereals and foodgrains enhance human peace and happiness? There are two aspects to it. These substances should be grown and then used properly. Herbs and foodgrains should be pure and wholesome to be fully beneficial for human health. How will that happen? By making the external environment for germination and growth of these herbs and grains pollution free. By maintaining ecological balance. By deriving good-quality seeds for germination and crop production.

The Vedic hymn next talks of the contrivances of comfort.

Look around and you will find dozens of articles of comfort. Mobile phones, air conditioners, automobiles, analgesics or pain-relieving drugs, synthetic warm clothing, sedatives, tranquilizers, etc.—all belong to the category of comfort-enhancing items. We need to look at whether these items are really enhancing net comfort of humans. Or are they just ameliorating pain and discomfort and bringing in more painful collateral effects of usage?

Human life is a set of cooperative and collaborative activities in which all the participants derive benefits—tangible or intangible. Human interaction—whether for agriculture, trade, industry, scientific research, space exploration or religious congregation and discourse—is some or the other type of yagya, in which all participants derive benefits. These activities need to in line with the principles of truth, transparency and moral propriety to enhance human peace and happiness.

Next, the Vedic hymn talks again of herbs and plants—the animate entities of the vegetable kingdom bringing us peace and happiness. These entities should get pure water and air and should grow in good-quality soil to be able to remain healthy and useful for us and other animals.

Havan kunda is the vessel used for the performance of *agnihotra yagya*. Oblations of pure herbs, ghee and other similar substances are made to the sacred fire in the *havan kunda*. The yagya is performed for the purpose of enhancing peace and prosperity. The yagya will be successful if the *havan kunda* is properly dimensioned and constructed to facilitate proper air flow, which will support and sustain perfect fire and enable complete combustion of the offered substances. The *agnihotra yagya* is a scientific process that will generate fumes to purify the environmental elements of air, water, fire, earth and ether and, in turn, enhance the peace of sentient beings.

Let us now see where and how the present practices deviate from the message conveyed by this mantra of the Vedas.

The modern world is privy to genetic tampering of plants, herbs, foodgrains and cereals in the name of quality and quantity improvement. This genetic engineering of vegetables, fruits and cereals is fraught with severe detrimental effects, which the scientists of the present times hardly realize. Purity of these products of nature means their natural integrity and wholesomeness. We are surely compromising with both in our modern scientific practice. We are violating the message of the Vedas. The choices are before us. We start following the message of the Vedas right now or we keep engaging in genetic engineering till we start experiencing catastrophic effects on a massive scale.

> *Organic farming has been shown to provide major benefits for wildlife and the wider environment. The best that can be said about genetically engineered crops is that they will now be monitored to see how much damage they cause.*
> —PRINCE CHARLES

It is unfortunate and deplorable that the pursuit of huge profits has led to the widespread investment, research and development efforts, propaganda and the resultant use of genetically modified crops, without adequate concern for the potentially hazardous effects of these crops on human health, and on the ecosystem and the environment.

Modern scientific pursuits have not spared even our water and air. Both are polluted and degraded. We need to restore their natural state by following the practices delineated in the

Vedas. Drinking water flows through the taps of RO filters, but the water still doesn't compare in quality with water stored in earthen pots. What is extremely serious is the fact that the entire practice of water management today is out of tune with the divine texts called the Vedas. Water-storage, water-handling and water-purification practices are leading to grave disturbance of the natural water cycle besides the huge pollution of water bodies caused by our industrial practices and handling of hazardous nuclear waste. This has to change sooner than later. The air around us now is perhaps more polluted than anytime in recorded or unrecorded history. The reasons are many—chemical industry, hydrocarbon burning on a mammoth scale, among others. These have degraded the air to dangerous levels. This cries for reversal. Our herbs and plants as also their seeds will be pure if the air and water fed to them are pure.

We still think of air as free. But clean air is not free, and neither is clean water. The price tag on pollution control is high. Through our years of past carelessness, we incurred a debt to nature, and now that debt is being called.
—RICHARD M. NIXON

The extent to which our callous handling of global water and air has degraded them in the last 200 years is amply indicated by the above quote.

We proceed to the next section of the mantra that deals with *havan kunda*—the vessel of the fire ritual prescribed in the Yajur Veda.

The purpose of *agnihotra yagya* done through *havan kunda* will be well-served if the ghee, herbs, seeds and fruit kernels consigned to fire are pure and wholesome. Their purity fundamentally depends on the purity of water, air and the soil. But unfortunately people dump non-biodegradable industrial waste on a massive scale in water bodies and soil.

Let us stop compromising with the purity of the various substances available in nature. It is going to cost us heavily.

We need to go back to the practice of the principles containing the pristine wisdom of the Vedas and their derivative texts on separate and specific subjects for our guidance.

The incantation of this divine mantra will invoke the blessings of almighty God to create conditions around us that will make way for enhancement of purity of natural elements and substances—something that is essential for overall peace and wellness, inner and outer. How exactly will it happen? It is our ignorance, illusion and arrogance that come in the way of enlightenment. The only way to have the scientific truths established is to invoke divine help from the greatest scientist—the omniscient Creator. This mantra of the Veda connects with Him for this purpose.

To the individual, this mantra gives the sublime message of preserving purity in nature. Let us not overly fiddle with air, water and soil. Let us maintain the natural constitution of things by avoiding unnecessary tampering with nature. The use of fruits and vegetables grown on soil treated with inorganic fertilizers and pesticides, the indiscriminate use of chemical-based drugs for human consumption and the big use of hydrocarbon-based automobiles are laden with baneful consequences and we need to curb these. Similarly, the use of natural substances after chemically refining them is fraught with harmful effects. The examples are refined petroleum products such as octane and diesel used as automobile fuels and plastic products for daily consumer use. Further examples that can be cited in this context are white sugar, white table salt, refined edible vegetable oils, chemical-based allopathic drugs derived from animal or vegetable sources and genetically modified foods. Splitting of atoms to produce nuclear energy and nuclear armaments is also a peace-disruptive process. Today, baneful effects of all such products and processes are slowly and surely coming to the fore. We need to take the divine cue from this mantra and correct ourselves in time without waiting for catastrophes.

EIGHT

Vibes of Peace from Terrestrial Elements and Spatial Directions

> *Aum shannah surya uruchakshah udeytu shannash chatastrapradisho bhavantu. Shannah parvata dhruvayo bhavantu shannah sindhavah shamusantwapah.*
>
> (May the brilliant sun which is the enabler of the process of human vision rise to make us happy. May all the directional and sub directional elements bring us peace. May the mountains, rivers and oceans bring us peace.)
>
> —RIG VEDA 7.35.8

The rising of the sun heralds a new day in the life of earthlings. The sun is the source of energy for humans and other sentient beings. This invigorating energy has to mix with true knowledge, hope, optimism and positivity to generate happiness. This energy has to combine with honest and pure intentions to work in a defined direction. This direction has to be in line with propriety and righteousness. Only then the energy from the sun will enhance our peace and happiness. This will happen when our sensory faculties including the sense of vision are involved in righteous karmas—karmas that will promote the welfare of all.

When the sun is shining I can do anything; no mountain is too high, no trouble too difficult to overcome.
—WILMA RUDOLPH

There are six directional elements—north, south, east, west, top and bottom. They represent the entire universe spread out in the ethereal space. These directions thus are representative of all the constituents of the vast universe. These constituents are the stars, planets, galaxies and constellations dispersed in space. How are these directions and human peace related? Our mind is a veritable antenna. It receives and absorbs thought signals from all directions. These thought signals alongside other types of energy signals carry profound effects on the mind. Waves of harmony and positivity impinging on the mind enhance peace, whereas waves of negativity disrupt it. People carrying anger, passion, hatred, fear, greed, lust and pride emit negative vibrations. These vibrations are disruptive of peace. Absence of these negative mental states is positivity. Positivity generates vibrations of love, stability and harmony.

The sub directional elements referred to in the Vedic mantra are the intermediate directions of north-east, south-west, north-west, and so on. The intent of this mantra is to reveal that we are closely connected with the entire universe through these directional and sub directional elements. We, the sentient beings inhabiting this universe, are closely interconnected.

The mountains, rivers and oceans are parts of the beautiful earth. The creator God has made everything on this earth with an intelligent purpose. The purpose behind this earth's creation was to provide a habitat to living beings, which are in essence the souls, to enable them to evolve through a gradual and incremental process of enlightenment.

The 8.4 million species of sentient beings are the creation of almighty God. They are the imperishable souls with bodies provided to them by the Creator.

Mountains bring water to earthlings in the form of rain or rivers. The latter originate at the mountains through its melting of snow. Rainfall as well as the flow of rivers need to be at the optimum or moderate level to be beneficial for humans. History is witness to famines and droughts caused by deficient rainfall, which have brought starvation and death to millions. And what happens when rainfall is excessive? The flooding of towns, streets and villages is being seen today more than any time in the recent history—thanks to the forces of climate change unleashed by the use of environment-unfriendly technologies and systems by ignorant people.

> *We are now in the mountains and they are in us, kindling enthusiasm, making every nerve quiver, filling every pore and cell of us.*
>
> —JOHN MUIR, *My First Summer in the Sierra*

Mountains are awe-inspiring objects of nature. They fill our minds with a natural zeal and a love for nature and the supreme Creator—the architect of it all. But today they have to bear the brunt of global atmospheric warming and the concomitant effects. The excessive or deficient flow of rivers and wind patterns are these effects, which bring troubles for the humans inhabiting the globe. The mountains and hills have also to bear the brunt of irregular real estate and infrastructure construction, often in flagrant violation of safety norms. The effects are only too evident in the recent episodes of hills and hillocks crumbling under torrential rains and carrying with them houses, temples and shops in the Uttarakhand state of India.

Rivers and oceans are the reservoirs of water. The havoc that swelling and flooding of rivers can cause to humans is well known. Sea storms, tsunamis, typhoons and cyclones are the phenomena caused by oceanic waters. Proper paradigms of living in line with the injunctions of the Vedas can prevent many of such catastrophic natural phenomena.

> *There was a magic about the sea. People were drawn to it. People wanted to love by it, swim in it, play in it, look at it. It was a living thing that was as unpredictable as a great stage actor: it could be calm and welcoming, opening its arms to embrace its audience one moment, but then could explode with its stormy tempers, flinging people around, wanting them out, attacking coastlines, breaking down islands.*
>
> —CECELIA AHERN

Our modern living systems comprising various types of industries have led to severe pollution of water in the rivers and oceans, the latter caused additionally by dumping of hazardous and non-biodegradable wastes. We are despoiling ourselves by partaking of such polluted water.

Right direction to human beings for right karma has to come from right knowledge. And the Vedas are the repositories of right knowledge. In order to promote noble, peace-promoting human karmas, we have to disseminate true knowledge revealed in the Vedas and their derivative texts. We need to educate global citizens about the primacy of Vedic literature, simplify the subtle messages contained in their cryptic hymns and spread them far and wide through the implements of modern technology such as the internet and mobile telephony. Today's global citizens are intimately connected through Facebook, WhatsApp, Instagram and other such social media platforms. It is easier to spread the truth today than ever before.

The prayer contained in this Vedic hymn has the power to tap the infinite beneficence of the almighty Creator for aligning our minds and intellects with Him so that we can draw motivation and true knowledge for peace and happiness. In specific terms, it will enable us to perform right actions that involve the handling of water—the vital basic element of nature. In other words, it will make our water-management practices truly scientific and align them with Mother Nature.

In a broader sense, invocation of the divine power of this mantra will help to generate and spread positivity all around. It will enhance peace of mind. And, above all, it will promote global peace and universal peace.

At the individual level, the chanting or practice of this powerful divine mantra works to improve our relationships with others. How does this happen? It works to make us more understanding, considerate and accommodating. It makes us more empathetic and caring. It tones down our temper and enables us to understand the truth better. Hence, it unmistakably works to improve our relationships—a major area of stress in life today. Better clarity of thought and a calm internal disposition will enable us to understand others' points of view better and hence become more empathetic. Internal calmness will create and strengthen bonds of love and friendship. Stress will obviously be diminished, for, a full 80 per cent of stress-related problems arise due to bad relationships emanating from faulty understanding of situations or people.

NINE

Peace through Learned Folks and the Almighty

Aum shanno aditirbhavatu vrateybhi shannobhavantu marutah swarkah. Shanno Vishnu shamupusha no astu shanno bhavitram shamavastu vayu.

(Our learned mothers performing good deeds, our erudite men and women with noble thoughts, the omnipresent creator Aum, our invigorating actions and this blowing air, may all bring us peace.)

—RIG VEDA 7.35.9

Our learned mothers are our preceptors, guides and indoctrinators. They are the ones who establish lasting impressions on our minds and hearts when we are young. They check us from going astray in our youth and they bind us to our family virtues and values when we have grown older. But the mothers have necessarily to be learned to be good guides for their children. If they themselves are lacking in knowledge and moral values, they can never be good and effective preceptors. Their own character in that case will be low. They cannot be expected to train their offspring on the right lines. And imparting right knowledge and sound values in youngsters is essential to their peaceful and progressive life.

> *Mothers are great. They outlast everything. But when they're bad, they're the worst thing that can happen.*
> —CARRIE FISHER

Our erudite men and women may be well-educated in the worldly subjects and domains, but they may not necessarily be people with noble thoughts. Nobility comes with acculturation. Those cultured people need to go beyond their individual closets of mind and beyond their self-interests to work for peace of the larger community and society. And peace will come only if their actions are in sync with the knowledge enshrined in the Vedas. It will come if they follow the tenets of universal dharma with a selfless outlook as mentioned above. It will happen when there is a welfare state or government administering the people and the latter are given the security of basic sustenance and healthcare.

However, the true scholars, who are like sages in wisdom and their actions, will always have a useful thing or two to teach us. We must respect them and be receptive to them. Only then can we benefit from their wisdom and deep knowledge. Where scholars are not revered, peace suffers a sure casualty.

> *One learns more from a good scholar in a rage than from a score of lucid and laborious drudges.*
> —RUDYARD KIPLING

The omnipresent creator Aum is also omnipotent, just and compassionate. We humans are free to act in the way we like or feel. We innately seek peace, fulfilment and happiness. But we are ignorant about many things. We have imperfect intellect and understanding. That is why we are liable to err. Out of sheer ignorance and sometimes due to frailty of mind, we violate the laws made by our Creator for the maintenance of harmony, stability and peace. As a consequence, our physical and mental wellness is undermined. We unwittingly disturb and disrupt peace, both inner and outer, by giving in to the pangs of passion, desire, lust and greed. We need the silent support and guidance of the Almighty to restore normalcy. This Vedic hymn connects with Him to make that happen.

Our actions can be passionate and invigorating for defined purposes. Those purposes could be noble or ignoble. As mentioned above, we could pursue ignoble causes mistaking them to be noble, out of sheer ignorance. Ignorance is illusory. This mantra of the Veda prays to the Almighty that we should channelize our energy for causes that will promote inner and outer peace. Prayer is required because of the inherently imperfect nature of human intellect. Prayer is powerful.

Finally, the mantra talks of the blowing air as the harbinger of peace. Blowing air can be the normal land breeze, normal sea breeze, a cyclonic gush or even a tsunami. It can be the cool and comforting breeze of summer evening or the devastating typhoon. Disturbing and destructive phenomena of weather are also the inevitable outcome of human violation of the laws of dharma established by the Creator. So in effect, the element of prayer in this mantra is an incantation that we remain aligned with dharma at all times so that the physical elements in nature do not have to show their destructive fury.

As mentioned earlier, the biggest indoctrinator and source of cultural grooming for a person is one's mother. How can a mother impart healthy culture and good values to her child when she herself lacks good education? How can she fashion good thinking in her children when she herself is steeped in ignorance or given to vicious habits? We need to look at this aspect of human life very closely.

Today's educated and erudite folks are seen using their knowledge more for promoting their own material interests than for the welfare of the larger community. This is a hard fact of today's world. Education lacks those elements of humanistic values that groom a youngster to develop into a person with a high degree of moral rectitude. We need to seriously review our systems of education across the world to make educational contents inclusive of basic humanistic values of truth, honesty and humility. These are far more important than the textual knowledge of engineering, medicine, economics, geography, accountancy or management.

The creator God is innately a peace-promoting power. But our actions attract equal and opposite retributive effects. If our actions are violent and violative of peace, there is no way that the just Creator will shower peace on us. We shall attract forces of disruption, destabilization and disharmony towards us. That suggests that our actions be peaceful in the first place. There should be no violence in our thoughts, speech or actions. What we find today is incidence of uncouth, disrespectful and even abusive speech. The Vedas declare that humans should speak the truth and speak it in a pleasant manner. Truth may be bitter, though. Angry and vengeful thoughts crowd our mental space. Such thoughts invariably translate into violent speech. And violent actions follow.

Our invigorating actions should bring us peace. What do we see in actuality? People's vigour and enthusiasm lie in overly ambitious actions that are out of tune with the established laws of the land. Their zealous actions are often laced with vengeance or greed. Their motive energy is directed in a big measure towards goals that are inconsistent with truth, transparency and universal welfare. The actions of closed, self-serving interest groups such as coteries in social communities, business houses and governments, actions of fanatic and fascist religious groups, actions of cartels in the world of trade and business and the actions of countries who join together to forge lopsided trade agreements such as General Agreement on Tariffs and Trade (GATT) surely exemplify the above. Such types of actions are not going to promote universal peace and welfare.

The blowing wind will bring us peace if it is carrying air free of pollution and not moving with a damaging intensity. That will happen when we deal with air as a vital element and in such a way that will preserve its purity and wholesomeness. That will happen when our activities and paradigms of living will be truly scientific and, accordingly, righteous.

Incantation of this divine mantra will invoke the infinite power of the Almighty to refine our intellectual faculties and bring our minds in tune with the realities permeating the universe. His beneficence is always available to us. It is our foolhardiness that comes in the way of tapping it. This mantra fills that gap, that void. This mantra also makes way for our interaction with the learned and saintly folks to benefit from them. Our actions will then become refined and righteous, thus enhancing peace and happiness all around. Once we start understanding things in the right perspective, we shall act prudently. Illusion and delusion will no longer exist. That means, we shall perform all peace-promoting actions. Ordinary human beings may perform regular chanting of this mantra for the desired beneficial effects.

TEN

Protection from the Radiant Sun; Beneficence from the Rulers

Aum shanno deva savita trayamanah shanno bhavantu shasovibhati. Shannah parjanyo bhavatu prajabhyah shannah kshetrasya patirastu shambhu.

(May the luminous sun protect us and bring us peace. May the clear bright dawns, the clouds and Shambhu, the lord of fields and territories, bring us happiness and promote our peace.)

—RIG VEDA 7.35.10, ATHARVA VEDA 19.10.9

The celestial object sun is the basis of all life and the source of its sustenance on earth. When will the luminous sun not protect us and enhance human peace? Think about the situations when people suffer from heat strokes and sunstrokes. Think about the hot scorching weather that brings diseases and discomfort. Consider the times when dry and hot climatic conditions parched agricultural fields and resulted in famines that took the toll of humans and animals by tens of thousands. Staring directly at the bright shining sun, especially during an eclipse, has permanently damaged the eyes of many people. All this happens due to our ignorance and us violating the laws of nature propounded in the Vedas. All this happens when we indulge in adharma or unrighteousness because the Vedas declare unequivocally that natural calamities and disasters are the result of humans violating the laws of dharma.

> *'Wow—I am really enjoying this 100 plus degree weather!'—said no one ever.*
>
> —UNKNOWN

The clear bright dawns should ideally be the harbingers of happiness for us. They should bring us good cheer resulting from the satisfaction of a day well spent and a natural desire to do better today with a sanguine outlook. But what happens in actual life situations? We frequently wake up carrying over the pangs of the previous day with its bad memories or even bad dreams of the night. We often get up with the hangovers and excess baggage of anger, sorrow and frustration. That brawl with the peer or that tiff with the spouse or that argument with the superior at work—all that had robbed us of our mental peace the previous day seem to trouble us the next morning too. Ideally, we need to improve on a day-to-day basis. What mistake we did yesterday should not be repeated today. That is what this Vedic mantra enjoins upon us to do.

Clouds have many functions to serve. One of these is providing rain and snow. They also help retain heat, like a blanket so it doesn't escape quickly into space. Temperatures on a cloudy night might be higher than on a clear starry night. On hot days, clouds provide shade. Clouds also serve to partly absorb and redistribute high-intensity radiation from the sun. The types of clouds visible in the sky provide an indication of the type of weather to come.

No doubt the phenomena of cloud formation are designed primarily to water the earth; to gather together the moisture from the salt sea, and form dark, unwholesome fens; to purify them by the mysterious alchemy of the sky; to carry them onward by sweeping storm or by gentle zephyr, and let them descend gently in the mist, or steadily in the rain, which will waken sleeping seeds, and revive drooping vegetation.

—ALFRED ROWLAND

Clouds bring rain, but they also bring acid rain—the fallout of a nuclear explosion as had happened after the bombing of Hiroshima and Nagasaki by the USA in August, 1945. Let human beings as the most intelligent creation of God perform such actions as will maintain stability and harmony of physical elements in the upper atmosphere. Let humans develop arms and ammunition or other warfare equipment that will be target specific, free of potential for collateral damage or environmental degradation. Nuclear armament developed in abundance today has all these defects. Such weapons should not be produced. That is the teaching emanating from this mantra of the Vedas.

Shambhu is the synonym of the creator God who as the permanent owner of terrestrial fields and territories will promote our happiness and peace if we humans follow the scientific principles of proper living as enunciated in the Vedas. If we abide by the eternal principles of dharma in our interactions with trees, tracts and terrestrial beings, we can never be troubled by any calamity or mishap nor shall we invite any sorrow in the form of disease, disharmony or dispossession. Our rulers act on behalf of the creator to dispense justice and promote peace in matters concerning ownership and usage of lands and fields.

In today's world, the term 'dharma' is the most misunderstood. In many instances, what is right for one community is held wrong for another. In the name of humanism and righteousness, there exist multiple sects. Some of the principles followed by one sect are decried by the other. If religion is meant to bring peace and happiness to society, then it must be applicable to all people irrespective of their location on this globe or elsewhere in the universe. In other words, religion must be universal. It must be based on truth and truth is revealed through the Vedas, the eternal scriptures of mankind, because the message of the Vedas came from the one and the only divine creator of humans. Repetitive reference to the Vedas is important because no scripture or text authored by humans can ever replace or supplant the divine scriptures that the Vedas are.

The modern world is witness to disturbed patterns of rainfall and river flow across the globe. In recent years, if we observed floods in the desert lands of Rajasthan, we also saw poor rainfall in areas of Assam which have otherwise received abundant rainfall for decades on. We have seen unprecedented heavy snowfall and devastating tsunamis, tornados, cyclones and typhoons at several locations on the globe. This has happened because we have been handling both air and water very indiscreetly.

Our water-management practices are out of tune with Mother Nature and we have been extremely harsh on the atmosphere, spewing millions of tonnes of harmful gaseous pollutants from automobiles, process industry units, thermal power plants and aviation vehicles every day. We have damaged the stratosphere. We need to reverse this damage by realigning our living paradigms with the injunctions of the Vedas.

During the last two or three hundred years, we have also not treated our tracts of lands well. Look at the way we have built our cities and indiscriminately destroyed forests. Today's urban areas are lined with large and swanky skyscrapers. They look like huge, spread-out concrete jungles. How we have made bore wells by the thousands over stretches of land and covered huge portions of those by concrete tiles or bitumen tarred roads is amply visible. We are unsure in what way these constructions are inconsistent with the working of nature and what could be their fallouts. But certainly our so-called scientific practices would cease to be scientific when it is discovered that they are not in line with the scientific principles prescribed in Vedic literature.

The incantation of this divine mantra will set in process divine undercurrents that will bring us in better tuning with the eternal peace-promoting laws of the universe. It will align our mind and intellect with the true scientific principles of the Vedas. It will open our eyes to the real truth of our so-called scientific techniques and processes and enable us to rediscover from our ancient knowledge base the true, environmental-friendly processes.

This alignment with truth and righteousness will purify our karmas which will result in us performing more humane actions and the use of sustainable techniques, technologies and processes. This will prevent vitiation of the basic elements of nature, thus preventing the outbreak of natural calamities. Our inner wellness depends on our physical and mental well-being. It will enhance both. We shall, by preventing violation of the immanent laws of nature, be enhancing our overall health and happiness.

ELEVEN

Peace from Knowledge, from Devatas

Aum shanno deva vishvadeva sham sarasvati sahadhibhirastu. Shamabhishachah shamuratishachah shannodivya parthiva shannoapyah.

(May all the devatas imbued with divine qualities enhance our peace. O Saraswati, the goddess of learning, may you bring us peace! These sages and savants, this ether, earth and water as elements, all may bring us happiness and peace.)

—RIG VEDA 7.35.11, ATHARVA VEDA 19.10.2

The devas/devatas referred to in this mantra are 33 in number. These are: eight Vasus (prithvi or earth, jal or water, agni, vayu, antariksh or ether, thyoulok or other world, chandrama or moon and nakshatras or constellations); 11Rudras (prana, apana, vyan, samaan, udaan, nag, kurm, krikal, devadatt, dhananjaya and jeevatma); 12 maas (months) (chaitra, vaishakh, jyeshtha, aashadh, shravan, bhadrapad, ashwin, kartik, margshirsh, paush, magh and phalgun); one Prajapati or yagya and one Indra or electricity.

All the above devas (or devatas) carry divine attributes and bring beneficial bounties to us. They provide to us without using these provisions themselves. The rivers and ponds do not consume their own waters. The sun does not use its heat and light but emits it for the sentient inhabitants of its planets. The moon brings cooling, soothing effect on humans. Its composure-giving energy is not for its own consumption. It is for our use and other sentient beings existing on earth. The eight Vasus are celestial abodes of living organisms.

The term 'thyou' refers to the celestial worlds other than the earth. The constellations bring us and other sentient beings astral energy. The 11 Rudras include 10 variants of the primordial air element that perform various functions in the human and animal bodies. The 12 months are the providers of climatic bounties in the form of objects and elements associated with different seasons—winter, spring, summer, monsoon and autumn/fall. The last two devas are Yagya—the activity that is the harbinger of all peace, progress and prosperity to humans and Indra, which is the prime functional element in the operation of human mind and intellect and is the charging agent of our 10 senses through which we perform all our earthly karmas.

The mantra in question has a prayer to the Almighty that our actions in the handling of the physical world may be such as will preserve the purity of the elements—air, water and soil and of the naturally grown vegetables, fruits and cereals.

Saraswati is the goddess of learning. Saraswati is a collective term used for all live or animate entities who educate and teach us. It also includes all material objects that help to enhance or upgrade our knowledge. Thus, our school and college teachers, private tutors, educational tools and kits, books and scriptures—all are covered by this term. To say that Saraswati may enhance our peace means that knowledge should be pure and uncorrupted. And so should be our knowledge givers—the teachers, scholars and academicians.

Sages and savants are people of knowledge, wisdom and righteousness. Their actions will be conducive to our happiness and peace when we are receptive to their suggestions and advice. When our own thinking is vitiated, when our own ideology is distorted, when our own attitudes are negative, we shall be unable to benefit from wise counsel. We, the ordinary human beings, need to be in the right frame of mind to absorb good ideas.

The ethereal space has all material objects of the universe contained in it. The ether has unique properties as a building element of material nature. It is the medium of communication of sound, of light, of high energy radiation and of astral waves. It is also the transmission medium of thoughts. But it is material in nature and subject to the laws of the material world, to the principles of physics and chemistry. Hence, the ether must retain its purity and wholesomeness too for flawless transmission of the above-mentioned types of signals. Human peace and well-being will depend critically on the purity of this vital primordial element.

The importance of maintaining the purity of earth and water as primordial elements has already been explained in previous chapters. The bottom line is that our working techniques and technologies as also our living paradigms must be in line with the principles enunciated in the Vedas. Look at the present ways. Almost all industrial systems that use minerals, ores and other raw materials result in finished industrial products that are either fully or partially non-biodegradable. Not only this, the industrial residues and waste products are dumped into water bodies such as rivers and sea, thus polluting them. Most of these waste products are non-recyclable too. Nature has an inherent mechanism for recycling of all materials—this being only too evident in the natural recycling of dead plants and carcasses of animals as also of the primordial elements viz. water and air. But our industrial processes that churn out any products that are not recyclable are outright non-scientific and will undermine human wellness.

> *The earth will not continue to offer its harvest, except with faithful stewardship. We cannot say we love the land and then take steps to destroy it for use by future generations.*
> —JOHN PAUL II

The mantra then talks of teachers and educators.

How do we rate today's educational systems under the reference framework of the Vedas? Education should be holistic and aimed at comprehensive development of the individual. It should promote physical, mental, intellectual and, above all, spiritual development of human beings. It should not be lopsided or narrow in its scope. It should not just groom and skill the person for specific avocation but also train him/her to perform his/her role well. But the present system of education, unfortunately, does not fulfil these criteria of Vedic philosophy. It produces literates but not necessarily well-skilled people. It churns out by the millions graduates and post graduates but does not develop in them a good moral sense. It produces doctors who treat patients but, in many cases, lack compassion. It produces good engineers and technicians, but they work as mere mercenaries. It creates teachers and academicians who do not think beyond syllabi, pass percentages and grades. It produces scientists who prefer to reinvent the wheel rather than tap the divine knowledge base of Vedic scriptures. It produces finance and management professionals whose sole focus is on profit. The list is pretty long. We need to correct these aberrations in our educational systems to bring them truly in line with the wisdom of the Vedas. The Vedic system of education is the ancient Indian gurukul system in which educational streams are broad based and holistic rather than compartmentalized. Such system will develop in students a quest to solve the riddles of life and a scientific temper. It will bring about holistic development of individuals.

I keep six honest serving men. They taught me all I knew. Their names were Where, What, When, Why, How, and Who.

—RUDYARD KIPLING

Establishment of a scientific and holistic system of education will, accordingly, be conducive to equity, harmony and peace.

Now cast a look at the so-called sages and savants or the god-men of today. So many of them with hordes of followers get implicated in serious crimes such as murder and rape. Bapu Asaram, Baba Rampal and Gurmeet Ram Rahim Singh are well-known examples in India who have undergone incarceration. Driven by greed and lust, such people become a curse on the society. Such types of religious men can bring peace and happiness to the masses only if they become better educated and enlightened, reject fake preachers and consecrate the genuine ones. This can happen only when the masses come out of blind following, blind faith and superstitions. This is possible when the common people understand and embrace truth—truth that is enshrined in the Vedas.

The above truth or true knowledge applied to ether, earth and water elements will promote peace of humans at all times. It will enhance peace by promoting purity and harmony. The mechanism is scientific and the process pertains to the working relationship between man and his physical environment, of which space or ether is an integral part.

TWELVE

Peace from Judiciary, Skilled Men and Parents

Aum shannah satyasya patayo bhavantu shanno arvantah shamusantu gavah. Shannah ribhavah sukrita suhasta shanno bhavantu pitaro haveshu.

(May the upholders of justice and truth bring us peace. May our wealth bring us peace and happiness. May the intellectuals and saintly people bring us peace. May our parents bless us with peace and happiness through our yagyas.)

—RIG VEDA 7.35.12, ATHARVA VEDA 19.11.1

The upholders of justice and truth—the judges of courts, the administrative officials of the government and the political elite whom they report to, the ministers and the prime minister or the president—are our governing elite. They are the dispensers of justice to the common people. They must do their job well. They must be people of integrity. They are the earthly representatives of God, who delivers perfect justice to all His human subjects. Perfect justice means that God's justice will fill gaps in the justice delivered by our courts. God's justice is seamless and timely. It is delivered subtly and silently. The process needs no courts, no lawyers, no petitions and no hearings because it is orchestrated by the omniscient and omnipotent Creator.

Our wealth must be earned legitimately to bring us peace and happiness. Wealth generated through questionable means brings misery and sorrow. This is an age-old axiom but hardly followed well in contemporary times.

Our intellectuals and saintly people will bring us peace when they are themselves attuned to the reality and dharma. They should be genuinely aligned with popular welfare. They should be of independent thinking and selfless. They should not be fraudsters, imposters or criminals.

Our parents will shower their blessings upon us when we respect them and obey them reasonably. When we live together under the same roof with our parents, we must serve them and do our utmost to satisfy their needs. Our parents will bless us when we fulfil their physical, mental and emotional needs.

Are the upholders of justice doing their job well in the modern world? Justice is often delayed and denied by our courts. More often than not, the makers of law, i.e. the legislators, make defective laws that do not serve the citizens well. Their actions are coloured by partisan thoughts. We do find plenty of instances where judges are not found to be above board. Judgments delivered by district-level courts are reversed by the high courts and high court judgments are reversed by the Supreme Court. We need to make our legal institutions more responsive to the needs of the justice seekers. Lawyers should work for justice to the plaintiffs and not just for their professional fees. There is plenty of money today with the law breakers, criminals and the corrupt. With money power playing its role in the legal process, justice often gets delayed and derailed. This is an unseemly situation.

Wealth will bring us peace and happiness only when it

is earned through right means. It will destroy our happiness when earned through corrupt or dishonest means. The law of karmic retribution operates subtly and seamlessly through the entire universe. Corrupt methods of generating money immediately disrupt peace within and ensnare a person in the retributive grip of his vicious karma. This simple understanding that foul means of wealth generation destroys inner peace will refrain and restrain a person from adopting them. This is the essence of this part of the Vedic hymn under discussion and analysis.

> *The thief steals from himself. The swindler swindles himself. For the real price is knowledge and virtue, whereof wealth and credit are signs. These signs, like paper money, may be counterfeited or stolen, but that which they represent, namely, knowledge and virtue, cannot be counterfeited or stolen.*
>
> —RALPH WALDO EMERSON

Today's world presents a grim picture of economic corruption and sleaze. You find individuals and institutions steeped in economic crimes. There are numerous methods of misappropriation of wealth. The dealings of government bureaucrats, bankers and businessmen are, in many cases, found to be shady and corrupt. Corrupt crony capitalism plays its part in the governance of many countries. In the macro picture, economic crimes occur on larger scales in the form of depredations of the weaker nations by the stronger ones brought by hegemonic ways. Colonial plunders of the past centuries are replaced by more subtle and covert ways of economic exploitation of countries. The World Trade Organization (WTO) regulations such as GATT have only served to increase the gap between developing countries and the developed ones. War mongering is another devious method of generating money through the sale of costly armaments and then involvement in reconstruction of war-ravaged areas. We need to understand in depth the divine injunction contained in this mantra of the Vedas and correct our ways and systems accordingly.

Intellectuals and saintly people will bring us happiness when we are rightly disposed towards them, when we are properly oriented towards them. Only in that case shall we be able to absorb good things from them. Today's world presents many high-grade intellectuals who lie neglected or unnoticed. Many of these intellectuals and genuine saints are not getting the respect they deserve. All this is entirely due to the apathetic behaviour of the common people. All this is attributable to the thinking and attitudes of the contemporary people who, out of their own illusory states, fail to recognize and value genuine intellectuals or true saints. So, what is needed is self-correction. What is required is mental purification and intellectual refinement. Incantation of this specific mantra of the Veda makes that happen.

> *One cannot possibly understand the teachings of the saints unless one has a pure mind and is trying to imitate their life.*
>
> —ATHANASIUS

The blessings of our parents carry powerful effects in our daily lives. In our yagyas, which are participative and collaborative activities, our parents' good wishes act as the catalysts that facilitate success. These good wishes or blessings work to increase positivity in our internal environment of heart and mind and also in our external environment. This positivity enhances our stamina and enthusiasm in the work undertaken.

But what is the condition of elderly parents today? In most of the societies, elderly parents are not well cared for and attended to. They are often found languishing in old-age homes and leading miserable lives. Even when living with their own children under the same roof, the elderly parents are neglected. We also come across rare cases of old and incapacitated parents being assiduously cared for and nursed by their children who are themselves in their fifties or sixties. It presents a great sight. Let parents in all situations be respected and cared for. Their blessings will then pour out profusely and work to the happiness and welfare of their children.

What is the practical message emanating out of this mantra for the common man? He/she must be impartial, unbiased and just. He/she must earn by means which are honest and do not infringe upon anyone's fundamental rights. He/she must be prudent in the choice of guides and gurus. He/she must be devoted to his/her parents because the parents' blessings are going to continuously promote his/her peace and prosperity.

What is required for the above? A strong mind and a clear intellect. Practise of this mantra through regular chanting does indeed provide the above twin benefits.

Let us briefly recount what really is the position today in the four areas touched upon by this mantra. People in large numbers are biased by their impressions, coloured opinions and preconceived notions based on indoctrination or faulty judgments. Such people are unlikely to be just in their dealings. Honesty sometimes appears to be a rare commodity, except in well-administered systems or at levels that are subject to intense scrutiny. People in huge numbers are being blinded and swayed by fake gurus and god-men. And finally, youngsters and even grown-ups in large numbers regard it unfashionable to follow their parents' advice. Respect or reverence for parents and devoted concern for them have clearly diminished. All this can change through clear perception and strong will. Practise of this divine mantra develops both.

THIRTEEN

Happiness from the Creator; Peaceful Navigation through the Oceans

Aum shanno aja ekapad devo astu shanno ahirbudhanya sham samudra. Shanno apaamnapaatperurastu shannah prishnirbhavatu devagopah.

(May God almighty, the never born, the all-pervasive, the giver of happiness bestow on us happiness and peace. May the clouds in the sky and the oceans bring us peace. May the space, which is protected by God, bring us peace. May the sea vessels and ships enable us to navigate safely and successfully.)

—RIG VEDA 7.35.13, ATHARVA VEDA 19.11.3

What is the function of the creator God in the vast universe? He controls and regulates the entire universe, which has been designed and made for sentient living beings to help them refine, develop and spiritually evolve. The universe with its planetary abodes presents a physical platform to those sentient beings. God is responsible for maintaining perfect justice in the universe and for the countless living beings inhabiting it. If we find someone to be unhappy and not at peace with themselves, certainly God has not bestowed on them peace and happiness.

What is the reason behind this? They have not helped

themselves. And, because, God helps those who help themselves.

How does a person help himself/herself to be happy and peaceful? He/she must be perseverant and make the best use of his/her time for positive, constructive and progressive activities. He/she must remain selfless, which means remain oriented towards the welfare of others.

May the clouds in the sky and the oceans bring us peace! The reader will observe certain incantations getting repeated in the Vedic mantras. The reason is simple. We humans are limited of knowledge, understanding and intellectual power. The concepts of God, nature and soul are esoteric and not easy to grasp. So is the understanding of the human mind and the way it gets influenced by the elements of nature. Apart from this, human memory is short. We learn something and tend to forget it the very next day. That is why important teachings get repeated in the Vedic mantras. Repetition ensures that the message gets lodged in the human subconscious mind.

As mentioned above, this Vedic mantra talks about the clouds in the sky and the oceans bringing us peace. Ancient scriptures derived from the Vedas declare that natural calamities such as torrential rains, sea storms and floods are the outcome of violation of the tenets of dharma by humans. Dharma, in its broad-based definition, includes assimilation and the use of true knowledge. This again points at the fact that violation of the tenets of dharma and application of half knowledge and unscientific or false knowledge lie at the base of natural calamities. True knowledge is that which is consistent with the Vedas. Broadly, dharma is that set of human actions which promote the welfare of other humans and other sentient beings. In the present times, glaciers are melting at a rapid pace, which means that the level of the oceans is gradually rising. This is creating potentially calamitous conditions on the globe. This is apart from the fact that we consider the vast oceans as a treasure bed for our exploitation or otherwise a dumping ground for wastes such as plastic waste or hazardous nuclear waste.

> *It is fashionable now-a-days to talk about the endless riches of the sea. The ocean is regarded as a sort of bargain basement, but I don't agree with that estimate. People don't realize that water in the liquid state is very rare in the universe. Away from the earth, it is usually a gas. This moisture is a blessed treasure and it is our duty, if we don't want to commit suicide, to preserve it.*
> —JACQUES-YVES COUSTEAU

'Space' is a synonym for ether, which has figured in the previous mantras also. The ether is one of the five cardinal gross elements carved out by the Creator from qualitative primordial matter possessing the three attributes satogun, rajogun and tamogun. The ether is the space that holds the prime building blocks of matter—the electrons, protons, neutrons, positrons and photons—in definitive arrangements creating shapes and sizes in the form of a variety of physical objects. The ether essentially contains in it all material objects. Yes, definitely, the ether physically holds and sustains all celestial bodies in the vast universe. The universe remains in stability and dynamic equilibrium because ether is protected and preserved by the creator God. Any disruption or disturbance to the wholesomeness of ether is bound to create huge disturbances in the inhabited worlds, seriously threatening the well-being or even existence of the sentient beings there.

The next prayer in this mantra is for successful navigation

across the seas through the use of marine vessels. Excessive turbulence in the seas again is the fallout of violating the principles of scientific living by humans. Scientific living here means living in accordance with the laws of nature as expounded in our Vedic scriptures. We have, in recent times, read about large marine cargo vessels getting trapped and sinking in the high seas. This is the result of technological deficiencies and operational lapses as much as the disturbed condition of the seas. All are within human control. What we call fury or vagaries of nature are not really natural phenomena that we cannot prevent or modulate. Vedic sciences show the way to maintaining the purity, balance and stability among the primal elements of nature, which include water and air.

To use the abundantly available power of God for our inner wellness, we need to tap it. We tap it through praise, prayer and meditative communion. The language of human communication with the divine creator is immaterial, the intention and emotion of the human subject is. The mode of worship is immaterial, the thought is. The infinite reservoir of beneficence and bliss is all around us. We often fail to take its cognizance. We should directly connect with Him and partake of the divine nectar that flows from Him to His human subjects. This divine nectar has the power to purge our mind of its impurities, brighten and sharpen our intellect and enhance inner peace. This is an eternal truth. One has to actually meditate upon God at any time to realize it. That suggests we should sit in meditation upon the creator God on a daily basis. The ideal time to perform this activity is early morning, before sunrise. Sit straight with your spine and neck erect. Draw a deep breath in and then slowly exhale. Then, with eyes closed, think of nothing else but the attributes of

God, who is omnipresent, omnipotent, just, compassionate and an embodiment of bliss. Do this for five to 10 minutes daily and see the difference.

What can a person do to derive peace and happiness through ether—the medium of sound, thoughts and other energy transmission? Cultivate a mindset of positivity. Think positive and talk positive. Spell or speak out clearly every morning and every evening what you truly desire. Do not speak out what you do not desire. Banish negative thoughts from your mind by imagining positive and favourable turnout of events. The ethereal space will transmit back at you positive vibes from all the directions through the vast universe.

As already mentioned in the explanation of the previous mantras, we need to preserve the natural purity and regional distribution of the environmental elements including water and air. If that is done, to a great extent, these natural elements will remain composed too and we will see less of torrential rains, storms, swollen rivers, cyclones and tsunamis.

What can an individual do to maintain the purity of water and air elements? Besides following the civic laws of pollution control, we should perform *agnihotra yagya* regularly. This yagya is a ritual in which oblations of pure natural substances such as ghee, cereals, medicinal herbs, dry fruits, etc. are offered to the fire (Agni) alongside recital of the divine Vedic hymns. It scientifically and subtly purifies water and air. Through this yagya, the power of nature works for peace and harmony of humans. Behind this power is the infinite power of the creator God. Apart from the above benefits, this yagya is also instrumental in purifying ether and preserving its wholesomeness. This preservation maintains stability in the physical environment. The modern world knows precious little about ether. Ether as a primordial element of nature needs to be studied scientifically and based on scientific study and analysis of this substance, we can develop scores of superior technologies which will be sustainable and maintain all-round stability and harmony.

FOURTEEN

Grace of Lord Indra for Peace and Joy

Aum Indro vishwasya raajati. Shanno astu dwipadey sham chatushpadey.

(O Lord of the universe, You are the master of this world. May all sentient beings derive peace and happiness through Your blessings.)

—YAJUR VEDA 36.8

God is the master of the entire universe. He is the permanent owner of material things. We humans who have limited lifespans are but temporary custodians of material objects, which could be anything—money, houses, properties, vehicles, bullion or any other assets. We hold onto them only during our lifetime, not after that. God is the creator of all celestial worlds and, therefore, He owns everything that these celestial worlds contain. He owns the basic raw materials as well as the finished products derived from them. This is so because the finished products are the creation of man and man in turn is created by God. Though the human soul is beyond creation, it cannot work on any material without its appurtenances—the body, the mind, the senses, the ego and the intellect. God has made all these appurtenances and fused it with the soul to create human beings. Hence, God is the master of it all.

Every sentient being innately desires peace and happiness. But it doesn't necessarily get them. With its limited intellect, it makes conscious efforts and performs actions to satisfy its desires, ward off dangers, overcome obstacles and prevent sorrow. But dangers do strike, problems do arise and sorrows do overwhelm the individual. This is often in spite of one's best efforts to attain happiness. That is where the necessity and role of God, the almighty creator comes in. Here comes the need of God's blessings and benediction. He is omnipresent, omnipotent and compassionate. He can and does assuage the sorrow of living beings who are His creation and His children. Worship of the Creator works subtly and scientifically, though it may appear to intellectually imperfect humans as being mysterious and miraculous in its working.

By incantation of this mantra, a person will be praising the overwhelming greatness of the creator God and also making prayer for peace. Praise of the almighty Creator refines a person comprehensively. It improves the thinking, disposition and habits of a person bringing him/her in alignment with sublime attributes of God.

Prayer assuages the pride of the individual and makes him/her more humble. Humility is the first requisite for a person to draw benefits from the almighty Creator. Pride and arrogance cost a person heavily in daily life. Because of them, one passes off into the illusionary state of self-righteousness and gets disconnected from many realities. Conversely, humility makes the person level-headed and in tune with the reality of situations.

Pride makes a person haughty and arrogant. It makes one argumentative and distances him/her from his/her less-endowed and perhaps less-fortunate peers. It deludes him/her into believing that he/she is super intelligent or super efficient or a super mortal compared to his/her less-endowed fellows. Blinded by vanity, one starts committing actions that are foolhardy and these same actions become instrumental in his/her downfall.

As stated above, prayer to the almighty Creator waters down our ego, making us humble and grounded. Once grounded in reality, we perform actions that facilitate peace and harmony. We tend to remain unruffled in good and bad situations. We grow calmer and more composed because of our own right actions.

> *When you do the right thing, you get the feeling of peace and serenity associated with it. Do it again and again.*
> —ROY T. BENNETT

What is the situation in the global society today? People in large numbers are afflicted by pride and superciliousness. You find arrogance in children as much as in adults and elders. One is not able to digest other's opinion easily. On public platforms, you find discussions laced with dissonance and disagreement. In discussions on public platforms sponsored by news media television channels—especially those related to politics, we observe sharp and acrimonious arguments. Representative of one political party hardly waits to hear other's point of view and begins to provide counterargument in an aggressive mode. The viewers get grumpy too.

The Veda in this hymn proclaims that the master of the world is compassionate and answers the prayers of His children. He blesses them with peace when they worship Him. Worship has three components—praise, prayer and meditation. It is prayer, as mentioned above, that brings humility in a person. Humility opens the door to enlightenment, peace and happiness.

Prayer messages of the Vedic mantras are not individual centric but are society centric or universal. When a sentient being is not at peace, it creates an aura of disturbance and this disturbance is passed on to other sentient beings in its vicinity. If a person is worried and tense, he/she depresses the mood of others also who interact with him/her or come in contact with him/her. That is the reason why Vedic mantras contain prayers for universal peace and harmony. All entities in the universe are interconnected.

What message does this hymn give to the individual human? Prayer to the Almighty for peace should be universalistic and not individualistic. The individual and the universe are inseparably interconnected through the medium of ether and through the medium of the universal spirit called God. Therefore, prayer for universal peace works better and more powerfully for the praying individual than prayer for individual peace. The universe operates through an immanent law of cause and effect set in by the Creator. If you create causes, there will be equal and similar effects. Prayer for peace is also a cause created which produces effect.

An experiment was conducted sometime back to gauge the effect of prayer for an individual vis-à-vis prayer for all individuals. Prayers were performed for the healthy growth of 10 individual herb saplings in a nursery and similar prayers were done in the context of a control group of 10 such saplings in a universal mode in the same nursery. In the universal mode, prayers were done for all saplings of the world. At the end of a month of regular daily prayers, it was found that the second group of 10 saplings grew better than the first group. It proved the point that prayers in the universal mode are more effective.

Pray for peace to all, pray for the happiness of all and

peace and happiness will come to you from the infinite reservoir of bliss that God is. This will happen in accordance with the inviolable law of cause and effect operating in the universe. The almighty Creator is the administrator of this law and He never fails to administer or apply it correctly. Hence, practice of this divine mantra will invoke the law of divine retribution for terrestrial peace, stability, harmony and security.

FIFTEEN

Moderation in Flow of Primal Elements

*Aum shanno vata pavatan shan nastapatusuryah.
Shannah kanikradaddevah parjanyo abhivarshatu.*

(Aum! O lord! May the blowing winds and the shining sun bring us peace and happiness. May the fire element and the clouds bring us peace.)

—YAJUR VEDA 36.10

The blowing wind is of varied types. It may be dry hot air of the summers, cold and heavy breeze of the winters, balmy gentle evening breeze, morning sea breeze of the coastal areas, dusty desert storm, cool breeze of the monsoon months laden with drops of rainwater, heavy gale, a cyclone, a tornado or a tsunami. Marvel at the sheer varieties of the terrestrial blowing wind.

The Vedas proclaim in clear terms that natural calamities of all types are due to adharma or unrighteousness, as has been expressed in one of the earlier chapters here. This adharma has a very broad definition indeed. It covers in its ambit all human deeds that are violative of the laws of nature. It covers all actions that are based on impatience and anger. It includes all dishonest and corrupt actions by humans. It also includes in its definition all actions based on imprudence and untruth. No doubt, it even covers all human actions based on wrong techniques, processes and technologies that harm the physical environment and disturb both ecology and climatic patterns. If humans follow dharma and shun adharma, natural calamities of all types can be prevented. Sounds strange and unbelievable and esoteric? Certainly it does! But it is true.

Loud wind, strong wind, sweeping o'er the mountains, fresh wind, free wind, blowing from the sea, Pour forth thy vials like streams from airy mountains, Draughts of life to me.

—DINAH MARIA MURLOCK CRAIK

The world has been made perfect and complete by the creator. The universe has been made perfect and complete. All celestial bodies are perfect and complete. And so are all living beings. So also is their ecosphere and the physical environment in which all these sentient beings live symbiotically. They live on different abodes—the celestial bodies. All of them are physically perfect—in structural and functional terms. Among the sentient beings, it is the human who is endowed with the best type of intellect and the knowledge of the Vedas from his creator with which he can refine himself to perfection and attain salvation. But our intellect and understanding are imperfect. We are liable to err. We apply the knowledge enshrined in the Vedas wrongly or incompletely in handling nature. Thereby, we end up spoiling or polluting or defiling the elements of Mother Nature. That is adharma committed. That sets in a negative retributive effect because that disturbs the normal rhythm and functioning of nature. When this situation becomes more serious, nature revolts and this revolt presents itself in severe climatic disturbances and natural calamities such as earthquakes or serious epidemics that takes human and animal lives.

Man, out of ignorance or out of weakness of character, also commits moral transgression. When such transgression happens in the form of inhuman karma on a wide scale covering huge human habitats, groups or communities, there occurs a severe retributive effect and natural calamity is one such type of retributive effect.

The supreme law of cause and effect operates eternally to maintain a balance in a dynamic mode. To use the terminology of physics, it maintains dynamic equilibrium in the universe. The prayer contained in this mantra seeks divine help for improvement in human karma so that degree of purity and stability in the elements of nature may improve. It seeks peace through refinement of human karma.

Let us review how the fire element called Agni is being used today for our benefit. The Yajur Veda says that fire element exists subtly in all matter as electricity. This fact is proven by the findings of modern scientists. They have been observing electrons and protons in atoms and electricity has been defined verily as the flow of electrons. We, the modern humans, have used electricity for multiple benefits. There is no doubt about that. The appliances and gadgets of daily use such as fluorescent lights, air conditioners, mobile phones, computers and microwave appliances all run on electricity. All types of industry—construction, manufacturing, surface transport, aviation or warfare—uses electricity in some form or the other.

We are so much dependent on electricity for our daily needs that our life without it is unimaginable. But look at the flip side of it. Electricity is produced on a large scale in thermal, hydro or nuclear power plants. Of late, the operations of all such plants have come in for severe criticism on account of their many harmful effects on the environment. So alternative, environment-friendly technologies such as solar or wind power generation plants are coming to the fore. Nuclear armaments are the most dangerous products of electricity. The world of today is sitting on a powder keg because of them. That is destructive or unwise usage of Agni. The Vedas condemn it.

What is the lesson emanating from the above?

We need to upgrade our technologies for generating electricity. Environmental protection is a greater priority. Global warming and climate change are threats to our very existence and survival.

> *The proper use of science is not to conquer nature but to live in it.*
>
> —BARRY COMMONER

In the context of the Industrial Age, not only has the proportion of carbon dioxide increased in the earth's atmosphere by 50 per cent since the pre-industrial times, but the pattern of rainfall and floods has undergone change too. Rainfall, both deficient and excessive, are visible geographical phenomena today. The parched desert land of Rajasthan in India witnessed heavy rainfall followed by floods a few years back. In the Cherrapunji area of Meghalaya, which is known for the highest rainfall globally, rainfall deficit occurred because of intensive deforestation. There are many more such examples. This points at our unscientific ways of dealing with nature—ways which are inconsistent with principles prescribed in the Vedas. We can change them or imperil our existence on this planet further. The choice is clear.

> *One of the first conditions of happiness is that the link between Man and Nature shall not be broken.*
> —LEO TOLSTOY

Vedic prayers work at the individual level too. So what does an individual gain from the chanting of this mantra? He will ameliorate the harmful effects of Agni. This Agni, which exists as digestive power in our belly, well get balanced bringing better health. Other adverse health effects of unbalanced Agni such as sunburns, rheumatoid arthritis, ulcers, pancreas and colon cancer, etc. will reduce too. Balanced Agni will also bring better mental health to the individual. The benefits are multifold. Chanting of this mantra will provide shield to the individual from the dangerous and calamitous effects of Agni. These effects include fire hazards of all types, electrical hazards such as electrocution and lightning and nuclear accidents as also the fallout of nuclear armaments. The protection shield provided by the Vedic mantras works at the most subtle level—at the level of the most powerful all-pervasive element that we call God almighty. We have to practise this to experience it.

SIXTEEN

Prayer for Success, Preservation and Lasting Peace

Aum ahani sham bhavantunah sham ratri pratidhiyataam. Shannah indragni bhavatamavobhi shannah Indravaruna ratahavya. Shannah Indra pushana vajasatau shamindra soma suvitayashanyo.

(May the day and night be peaceful for us. Our protector, Indra; the provider of all beautiful things, Agni Dev; the god of peace, Varun Dev; and the bestower of success, Som Dev and Pushan, may you provide us with wealth, mental tranquillity, success and protection.)

—YAJUR VEDA 36.11

We spend our days and nights quite differently. The days are spent in physical and mental activities of all kinds, while the nights are spent in rest and sleep. Night is a period of inaction. During the day, we perform all sorts of chores—domestic, professional and social. This hymn prays to the creator God for our peaceful performance of all work. What does the term 'peaceful performance' actually convey?

Since peace is a multi-meaning word connoting calmness, harmony and purity, we need to understand how our work performance can have harmony, calmness and purity. By harmony is meant congruity, consonance and compatibility with the surroundings. It shows a situation of an unruffled mind. That can happen when there is mutual acceptance among people and the element of anger or irritation is absent. Calmness is the state when the mind is free of worry, tension, stress and fear. This condition cannot exist when things for a person are not moving in the desired direction. Purity is the state of the mind free of impure thoughts such as hatred, jealousy, greed, passion and pride.

Now you can realize how comprehensive and all-encompassing Vedic hymns are. They cover each and every aspect of the human being. One can understand the superlative quality of work of a person when he/she does that work in a state of mind which is calm, pure and harmonious with its surroundings.

We need peace at night-time also for sound sleep and to recharge our body and mind. You cannot get sound sleep in a state of anxiety. You cannot get good sleep when in illness. In the present times of unnatural lifestyles, sound sleep is not a common feature of peoples' daily lives. People consume sleeping pills on a regular and routine basis to induce sleep. The mantra prays to God for sound sleep.

> *You'll be the last thing I think of before I fall asleep and the first thing to think of when I wake up.*
>
> —ANONYMOUS

God has multiple names and attributes. Indra is the protector and Agni is the provider of all beautiful things. Varun has been referred to as the lord of peace. Som Dev and Pushan have been named as the powers behind bestowal of success. Indra means the owner of all things and being Indra, God protects our earthly belongings. Agni means effulgent and the source of energy in all matter. God is the power behind the kaleidoscopic beauty of all worldly things and objects. The name 'Varun' means superlative and the best. This attribute attaches to God through the name 'Varun'.

Superlative quality of the creator God is instrumental in establishing peace and harmony, because for an entity to be able to establish peace, it must know the minds of the intelligent people and should have control over them. God is such an entity. But this condition is not enough for the establishment of peace. The entity must exist everywhere and should be all knowing. Again, only God is such an entity. These superlative attributes of the Creator—of Him being omnipresent, omnipotent and omniscient—play their role in the establishment of peace and that is exactly what this mantra is bringing out.

Som Dev is the god of peace. This is another attribute-based name of God. What is the meaning of 'Som'? It is the nectar of immortality. God is presented in Vedic literature as a spiritual substance and the source of the purifying nectar for humans during meditative communion. That purifying nectar has the property of purging the human mind and intellect of impurities. When the intellect begins to get refined and the mind begins to get purified thus reducing passion, anger, greed, attachment and pride, human beings move towards immortality, which is another term for salvation.

Pushan is yet another name of the creator God which literally means 'guide' or 'facilitator of progress'. God is indeed the prime facilitator of human progress. That is why this mantra talks of prayer to Pushan for success in worldly endeavours, especially those pertaining to wealth creation.

We all suffer from stress. The level of mental stress has increased remarkably in recent times. People's material expectations have become more. Peoples' expectations from life itself have increased. And that perhaps is the root cause of high stress levels. The famous industrial and business magnate Ratan Tata is quoted to have said—'Life is too short to be taken very seriously.' We give seriousness to everything in life because we start attaching the expectation of result to our every action. That creates stress. Performing our duties without expecting any reward in return is the best antidote to stress. We have control over our actions, but not over the reward. So there is no point stressing over it. We should accept this as a fact.

We also feel insecure, as we don't know what is going to happen the next moment. We want security of wealth and other material possessions, security of health, security of life. We want protection. We, on our own part, try to do everything to protect ourselves and our belongings. But the environment and future are loaded with uncertainties. We need protection from our supernatural creator. This Vedic mantra talks of exactly that. Repeated chanting of this mantra invokes the power of that infinite reservoir of bliss and benevolent power. It works because that infinite entity called God is compassionate and answers the prayers of His subjects. He protects them from dangers and adversities.

> *In security analysis the prime stress is laid upon protection against untoward events. We obtain this protection by insisting upon margins of safety, or values well in excess of the price paid.*
>
> —BENJAMIN GRAHAM

Protection, therefore, has a price to be paid for. That price may be additional conformity or adherence to values or prayer to the divine power that is.

This is an excellent mantra for bringing sound sleep. These days, quality as well as quantity of sleep has taken a dip. Medical experts issue daily advisory messages on the dangers of sleep deprivation. Sleep deprivation has been linked with ailments such as Parkinson's disease, Alzheimer's disease and even cardiac ailments. Daily chanting of the mantra for a duration of five to 10 minutes before bedtime will appreciably improve sleep. Chanting of this mantra will help to align the intellect and mind with existential realities and make a person better focussed in his work, thus improving his chances of success in endeavours of life. It also provides insurance against unknown dangers. Its protective power too works at the subtle, spiritual level, like that of any other mantra.

SEVENTEEN

God's Blessings for Happiness and Fulfilment of Desires

Aum shanno devi rabhishtayey aapo bhavantu pitayey shanyorabhisravantu nah.

(May the gracious, all-pervading God—the provider of bliss, grant us our wishes! May He shower peace and happiness on us from all sides!)

—YAJUR VEDA 36.12, SAMA VEDA 13.4.3

This is a great mantra that finds place in the Yajur Veda as well as the Sama Veda. How do we fulfil our many desires? Obviously, by working towards them. But we humans are mentally frail. We are intellectually imperfect. We often unwittingly take the wrong direction and land up in a mess. There is the other situation too that drags us away from our goalposts. We know the pathway to success but are unable to tread it due to our own laziness, lassitude and mental weakness. We are simply unable to persevere. So what should we do?

We have to lean on our creator God—the infinite reservoir of all positivity, all bounties, of compassionate power. We have to connect with Him, pray to Him.

> *We are not at peace with others because we are not at peace with ourselves, and we are not at peace with ourselves because we are not at peace with God.*
> —THOMAS MERTON

We need to understand what bliss is. It is the state of ultimate happiness and fulfilment. Bliss is not the state when some human desires have been fulfilled only to be replaced by more and bigger desires. It is not the state when human desires are partially fulfilled and the person remains unsatisfied carrying the burden of those desires. Desires have to be completely fulfilled or destroyed. There should be no remnant desires. Along with zero desires, another important condition is to be satisfied to achieve bliss. That condition is zero propensity to adharma. When a person reaches a state marked by absolutely no tendency to unrighteous, immoral or sinful conduct, he/she commits no action that will bring him/her grief. Thus, when the above two conditions are satisfied, a person attains lasting divine bliss.

God is the provider of bliss because God has control over the human mind, human intellect and human soul.

Peace and happiness from all sides connote a situation of perfect harmony with the surroundings. It is a situation when you have no enemies or detractors. It is a set of circumstances marked by positivity and optimism, by absence of fear or doubt. The absence of doubt means complete faith and conviction in the powers that are controlling and regulating the universe every moment. This faith, when it is strong, indicates that the person is well in tune with the universal harmonizing power that is an infinite reservoir of peace and happiness. This tuning provides for channels through which flows the divine nectar from God to His human subject.

This is the harmonizing nectar. This is the peace-promoting nectar. This is the immortalizing element.

Let us do an honest review of our present situation, both external and internal. Are our minds at peace or ill at ease? Are we carrying the pangs of disconnect with others with whom we should, otherwise, be having harmonious relationships? Are we having relationship issues with the spouse, boss, parent, classmate, playmate, professional peer, neighbour? Are these issues at the back of our mind always? Are they torturing and tormenting us while seated in our subconscious mind? Are these issues undermining our working efficiency and happiness? If the answer to these questions is yes, we seriously need to address the issues. How do we do it?

We should get connected with the almighty Creator. We should understand our relationship with Him. We should understand that we are His subjects and supplicants of His kingdom and court. He is the supreme owner and controller of things. He is just and compassionate. He dispenses perfect justice to His human subjects, because He knows everything. He needs no evidence, no witness to deliver justice. He is witness to everything. He wants to help His subjects grow—through learning and experience. He is all powerful. That is why prayer to Him works and it works wonders. The power of prayer is not adequately understood. It is far more than we believe or imagine it to be. When we are stricken with fear, anxiety, worry or depression, connection and communion with God help to assuage our stress. It is the greatest stress buster that can be. Communion with Him and prayer to Him give us the mental composure to better handle our relationship issues.

We human beings have wishes and desires. It is these desires that propel us forward and enable our experiential growth—spiritually. In the process of this growth, we blunder and commit errors. We stumble and fall, only to rise again with renewed vigour, driven by faith in our benefactor God.

The mediocre student wants to get high grades in his academic coursework; the chronic patient desires cure of his debilitating ailment; the cricket player dropped from his national test team desires to be selected again; the pauper desires to roll in money; the employee seeks a promotion and a raise; the businessman seeks higher revenue and profit margins; the politician in power seeks re-election in the next term. The list goes on. Fulfilment of desires will, for sure, bring satisfaction and happiness. The mantra under discussion seeks fulfilment of all human desires. It seeks the banishment of all sorrow. It is the instrument of tapping the all-pervasive God for all-round happiness and success.

Modern life is complex. We are living on many fronts simultaneously—family front, professional front and social front. Every human being plays multiple roles—that of a father or mother, brother or sister, relative, professional peer, workplace superior, workplace subordinate, employee, employer, neighbour, business customer, friend, teacher, student, doctor, patient, et al. Things, generally, are not expected to run smoothly on all the life fronts—by the sheer law of averages. But in this mantra, we seek the smooth run of all our life activities—the way we desire them to. Chanting of this mantra will make it happen.

Chant this mantra regularly for 20 minutes every day and you will see palpable changes in your life. It will make you both positive and realistic in regard to your expectations from life. It will make you prudent and perseverant. It will make you humble and polite, thus improving your relations with all. It will make you forbearing in adversity. It is bound to make you level-headed in approach. It will give you mental equanimity. It will give you a mindset to view adversity as an opportunity to grow and improve. Then where is the doubt that happiness will come to you from all quarters?

Each mantra in the Vedas is unique. Coming from the realm of the Almighty, the mantra described in this chapter carries specific vibrations that leave a positive effect on your astral body. Since the astral body consists of the conscious mind, subconscious mind, intellect and ego self, all these elements are thereby positively impacted. It will moderate and modulate your desires, bringing them in alignment with the reality. It will prevent situations of deep discontent and disappointment. A powerful life-elevating mantra!

EIGHTEEN

Comprehensive Prayer for Inner and Outer Peace

> *Aum dyaou shantirantarikshagwam shanti prithivi shanti rapa shantiraushadhayah shanti vanaspatayah shantirvishvey deva shantir brahma shanti sarvagwam shanti shantireva shanti sama shanti redhi; aum shanti shanti shanti aum.*
>
> (May there be peace—in the celestial world, in the ethereal space, in the earth element; in the water element. I pray for peace in medicinal herbs, in vegetation and plants, in all the learned and erudite people; peace in knowledge and peace generally everywhere. May God bestow on me such peace!)
>
> —YAJUR VEDA 36.17

This is the prime mantra for peace provided in the Vedas. The mantra talks of peace and translates as above.

Peace is its own reward.

—MAHATMA GANDHI

Peace in the celestial world connotes peace in all the extra-terrestrial bodies that exist in the universe. Definitely, there exist other planets like the earth where living beings dwell.

This mantra prays for peace to all those beings. It also talks of peace in planets not inhabited by living beings, in luminous stars such as the sun and in the natural satellite bodies such as the moon.

Remember and recall that peace being a multi-meaning word means calmness, stability, harmony and purity. These terms have to be applied to various sub contexts where the word 'peace' comes in this Vedic hymn.

The hymn or mantra then talks of peace in the ethereal space. The entire universe is filled with ether. Ether is a primordial element which is physically the space that contains all material objects of the universe. Peace in the ethereal space means calmness and purity in this element. This may sound a bit abstract, but it is scientific because it comes from the realm of the all-knowing Creator, who is also the greatest scientist.

Peace in the earth element connotes a condition in which the primeval earth element remains stable and pure. It remains in harmony with the other cardinal elements—ether, water, fire and air. Stability of this element is a condition in which landscapes and landslides will not occur; volcanoes and earthquakes will not occur. Its purity implies its property to hold the huge variety of flora and fauna—in their natural and healthy condition.

When there is peace in the water element, it remains free of contamination. Its distribution on the planet remains normal and healthy. Ponds and lakes do not dry up. Glaciers do not melt excessively. Ocean levels do not rise. Torrential rains do not come. Water-borne diseases do not strike humans and animals. Tsunamis and cyclones do not occur.

Peace in medicinal herbs means their purity. The worst thing that can happen to human beings inhabiting the earth is the dilution of the purity of natural medicinal herbs. Most of the medicines that are used to treat human illnesses are directly or indirectly derived from these herbs. If because of pollution of air, earth and water, these herbs lose their purity and efficacy, it will spell doom for us. That is the reason why prayer for preservation of purity of medicinal herbs and plants is contained in this divine mantra.

Peace in vegetation and plants also means their healthy condition. If the condition of vegetation and plants does not remain healthy, the animals feeding on them will become sickly too. Consequent upon this, the entire ecosystem will be disturbed. Human beings are part and parcel of this ecosystem. They will also be adversely affected.

Next comes peace in the context of learned and erudite people. The mantra prays for peace in learned and erudite folks. This peace connotes their healthy state of body, mind and intellect. If the learned folks stay healthy, they will contribute far more to the betterment of humanity. They are the most valuable class of the society because they are the instruments of advancement of knowledge. They are the vehicles of progress, as they work for the correction of social ills. They are inclined to work selflessly to rid the society of ignorance, obscurantism and the evils generated by them.

The greatest importance of peace is in the context of knowledge. Peace in knowledge refers to purity of knowledge. Unfortunately, it is knowledge which, in the present times, is most corrupted, polluted, distorted and also misrepresented and misinterpreted. What happens when knowledge is corrupted, wittingly or unwittingly? It leads to all-round deterioration. Human values are turned upside down. Truth suffers a body blow. Humans are driven into delusion. The distinction between right and wrong is thinned. Righteousness gets a jolt and the efficiency of human institutions to deliver progress and justice is reduced. Concepts become hazy and instead of ideology based on truth, disparate ideas and arguments crowd human discourse. So, the importance of core and fundamental knowledge remaining pure is extremely high.

In popular parlance, the term 'peace' everywhere means a state of calmness, serenity and tranquillity all around. It means absence of disturbing noise. It means absence of disharmony and instability. Peace is the state of harmonious human relationships. It is the condition of no stress. It is the state of sound health of mind and body.

> *The life of inner peace, being harmonious and without stress, is the easiest type of existence.*
> —NORMAN VINCENT PEALE

The mantra ends with the prayer for peace of the above-mentioned types for the individual human in relational setting with his creator God.

It is not difficult to see that the present world is witness to all-round erosion of peace. The fundamental divine knowledge for healthy human sustenance, development and salvation enshrined in the Vedas lies relatively neglected today partly because of deficient faith and partly due to erosion, in a large measure, of Pali Sanskrit—the original language of the Vedas. Derived scriptural texts, with dilution and distortion of the original strands of Vedic knowledge, are being followed. Driving knowledge in the fields of politics, economics, healthcare, education, trade or industry is not pure or in line with the core divine knowledge of the Vedas that comes from the omniscient Creator. In the area of science and technology, humans reinvented the wheel and worked their way forward based on incomplete or half knowledge instead of following the strands of true knowledge contained in the Vedas or their pure derivative texts. That led them to developing technologies harsh on the environment. This is starkly visible today with the governments struggling against the effects of environmental pollution and global warming.

If we had followed the technology of airplane construction as specified in Maharishi Bharadwaj's *Brihad Viman Shastra*, an ancient Hindu text derived from the Atharva Veda, we would have had noise-free, pollution-free airplanes that run on water, mustard oil, mercury or other simple substances. Such airplanes can still be developed. If we humans had followed Ayurveda in health management, we would not have so many chronic, intractable ailments such as cancer, Alzheimer's or AIDS. If humans had followed water-management practices prescribed in ancient Hindu texts, no water crisis would be looming large today. Half knowledge is a dangerous thing. Corrupted knowledge is far more dangerous.

Man has defiled his habitat by his ignorance and foolhardiness. All is not lost. We can revert to truly scientific practices of living which are in line with Vedic literature and overcome all problems.

Let us review and refine all modern practices, all the present techniques and technologies to make them nature friendly and pollution free. Protection of environment should get prime priority.

Chanting of this comprehensive peace-promoting mantra at the individual level is bound to ameliorate inner stress. It is a peace-promoting potion that will help to establish mental composure. It will be of great help in resolving relationship issues. It will help the individual to successfully tap the divine source of peace and serenity that has a universal spread to enhance his own inner wellness.

Practised at the collective level, this mantra carries the profound power of enlightening humans towards superior systems, practices and technologies. This will transform the character of institutions for the better and bring forth healthy living paradigms and processes to help restore purity of water, air and soil and re-establish ecological balance.

NINETEEN

Prayer for Longevity, Health and Freedom

*Aum tachhakshurdevahitam
purastahchhukramuchcharatta pashyemasharadah
shatam; jeevema sharadah shatagwam, shrinuyaam
shradah shatam, prabravaam sharadah shatamdinah
syaam sharadahshatam; bhuyascha sharadah shataat.*

(O Lord! You are witness to everything. You are the eternal friend and well-wisher of the learned folks. You were present even before the creation of this world. May we live for hundred years—under your command; may we hear for a hundred years and sing in your praise for hundred years. May we lead active working lives lasting a hundred years. May we live in freedom, without bondage all along. May we live like that even if we cross a hundred years.)

—YAJUR VEDA 36.24

Only the creator God is present everywhere and is witness to everything. That is why the Vedas say that He has a hundred eyes and a thousand ears. He is the friend and benefactor of all learned and saintly people. He supports them and helps them in their noble pursuits. He is eternal, unborn and immortal. He created all the worlds of the vast universe. So, He was present even before the creation of the world and will remain after the dissolution of the universe. The prayer in this mantra is offered to such omniscient, omnipresent, omnipotent, eternal and timeless entity who created us. It prays to Him that we live for a hundred years. This part of the prayer shows that He protects us from dangers and calamities—and untimely death. He has fixed the normal human lifespan as a hundred years. While living for a hundred years, may we continually sing in His praise.

What happens when humans sing encomiums for the Almighty? They begin to absorb God's divine qualities. They start becoming like Him—just, compassionate, truthful. Their deficiencies and drawbacks decline. They start getting refined.

The prayer further goes thus: may we humans be free from bondage and spend a hundred years in such freedom. Freedom is the prime requisite for human fulfilment and salvation. Freedom gives a person the proper perspective for spiritual growth. Hence, freedom is important. The mantra finally says that even if we live beyond 100, we may live in freedom and with our senses of hearing and speaking intact.

The mantra, in brief, contains prayer for a long life and quality life.

Why is a long life of hundred years important? Because the purpose of our life is experiential learning, fulfilment and ultimately salvation.

> *A long life may not be good enough, but a good life is long enough.*
>
> —BENJAMIN FRANKLIN

Every stage of life holds its own unique importance for the above learning. Experiences of human life as a student, as a householder, parent and professional and as a recluse in renunciation are important in their own unique ways, contributing to learning and spiritual refinement. The objective of human existence is essentially spiritual refinement and transcendence. As a child and student, a person learns how to deal with parents and preceptors. One learns the value of respect, of knowledge, of transparency, of truth and of parental love. In adolescence and youth, one learns the tenets of friendship and companionship. One gets ample situations to understand the importance of discipline and of perseverance.

In middle age and as a householder, a person learns experientially the values of justice, fairness and compassion. His/her daily grind of domestic and professional chores makes him/her even more disciplined and hard working. So his/her understanding of the importance and value of perseverance grows further. In old age, a person realizes the value of health and the limitations of wealth. His/her bloated self-importance shrinks and he/she grows more humble, because he/she has understood that it pays to shed arrogance and that high self-importance was an illusory feeling.

Towards the end of one's life, all worldly life experiences tend to make the person detached and kindle or consolidate his/her faith in the divine. It is during this phase of life that atheists become believers and borderline believers called agnostics develop strong faith in God. So human life of a hundred years is necessary for complete human development.

But is a life of hundred years desirable if considerable portions of it are spent in pain, privation or penury? Is the life worth living with vision fully or partially impaired due to any reason? Is life enjoyable if hearing power is lost? Or if limbs are incapacitated due to disease or injury? Does life retain its charm if we have to struggle with chronic, intractable or incurable disease that makes us depend on others for livelihood or sustenance?

It's a real roller-coaster ride if you're lucky to have longevity in this business—you have to be able to ride those waves.
—JENNIFER LOPEZ

It is our earnest prayer to the almighty God to protect us from all calamity and all misery. May we, through His blessings, remain physically and mentally fit ever. May we remain self-sustaining and also fit enough to help the needy and the deprived. This mantra of the Veda seeks divine benediction for all this.

Freedom is the birth right of every sentient living being. Lock a parrot in a cage and see how it struggles to free itself and fly out. Chain a pet dog and confine it in your house to see how it seeks freedom and wants to follow you whenever you leave your house. We do not like bondage too. Bondage of any kind—physical or economic—is anathema to an individual. It is in freedom that the living soul asserts itself, expresses itself and learns through experience. In the process, it refines itself. Freedom is truly an essential requisite for human development and salvation.

The present Vedic mantra prays to the Almighty for freedom. It prays to Him that we may live for a hundred years singing encomiums for Him. Our connection with the Lord is necessary for us to lead optimal existence—both physically and mentally. We need His support and His protection all through. His protection, support and benediction are indispensable. He fills the gaps in our knowledge and understanding. He helps us to tide over the moments of crises in our lives by making us face challenges with courage and fortitude. Faith in Him is the most powerful instrument through which a person is able to overcome fear, depression and lethargy.

The mantra carries divine effects for providing protection against illness to a person. The secret of long life is moderation and mental discipline and the secret of good health is the knowledge of principles of healthy living and their due application. Regular chanting of this mantra builds up mental discipline of a person. It mystically protects a person from accidents and injury. It creates healthcare awareness in him/her.

What message does this Vedic hymn carry for humanity?

The modern world is overly commercialized. In every activity we perform, we see the commercial angle. No one bothers the other without some material interest. Selflessness in action and behaviour seems to be on the wane. The healthcare and pharmaceutical industry thrives on false information and propaganda. The focus of medical practice is not on cure of illness but on management of illness. This management sees more and more drug consumption, more diagnostic tests and frequent visits to clinics and hospitals with complications rather than cure of illness. This is an unbecoming situation and quite unfortunate too.

The application of the timeless principles of Ayurveda holds the key to successful healthcare. And Ayurveda emphasizes on prevention rather than cure. Assiduous adherence to the principles of Ayurveda in daily life can prevent disease in a big way. Even the treatment of diseases in Ayurveda is cheaper and qualitatively far superior. Thus, following Ayurveda in healthcare and medical practice can save the world billions of dollars in healthcare. That is what we should be doing, really. That is the way we can improve both human longevity and quality of human life on this planet.

Practising this mantra will enhance our understanding of the true philosophy of healthcare, of the timeless principles of Ayurveda and, at the same time, increase our willpower so that we can apply these principles in our life for gains in health and longevity. Further, as already stated in the foregoing lines, the divine mystic power of this mantra provides protection to its practitioner from catastrophes and calamities. It gives us the time and space to expiate our past karmas and fulfil our desires and in the process, refine ourselves through all the valuable experiences that a hundred years of sentient existence can provide.

TWENTY

Noble Aspirations for the Wandering Mind

Aum yajjagrato duramudaitidaivam
tadusuptasyatathaivaiti durangamam jyotisham
jyotirekam tanmey manah shivasankalpam astu.

(The human mind wanders rapidly while we are awake or asleep. This mind is the driver of all senses. May my mind be filled with good thoughts and harbour noble determinations.)

—YAJUR VEDA 34.1

The mind is the most important non-spiritual entity in the human being. It is, by its very nature, excitable, sometimes fickle and of wandering type. It doesn't stay fixed and focussed on any subject for long. The mind rapidly carries thoughts of different shades and colours. It takes one moment to transport us from earth to Mars and another moment to bring us back. This wandering tendency of the mind has been likened to a monkey who jumps from one branch of a tree to another. The mind behaves like this when we are awake. But in sleep also it harbours dreams with multiple trains of thought.

The mind is the single most important material entity in the human body, as mentioned above. It is the controller of senses—five cognitive senses (smell, taste, sight, touch and hearing) and five functional sense organs (hands, feet, tongue, excretory organ and reproductive organ). All that we do in terms of functional karmas is controlled by the mind. Functional karmas include thoughts, speech and actions through the functional sense organs.

The mind should be in a sound state for the good performance of these karmas. What does this sound state signify? It signifies that the mind should be free from clutter, confusion, fear and illusion. That matters a lot.

But more importantly, the mind should have noble intentions, aspirations and determinations. If you desire to achieve some life objective, you should be determined to achieve it. Whether that noble goal is an invention that will benefit humanity, developing a medicine for cure of some serious ailment, winning the world cup for your country in international hockey, getting admission in the preferred graduate school of your choice, developing a technique of successful agriculture in semi-arid and arid zones of your country, propagating the message of truth and humanism contained in your religion, fighting against sex-discriminatory practices in your society, living a disease-free life of a hundred years or any other noble aspiration for your individual good or for the larger welfare of your community—all these noble goal realizations are the results of determinations set in the mind.

Determination is the key. The mind is your power centre. It must be focussed with steely resolve to win. Nothing can then stop you on your way to success, achievement and glory.

Men are not prisoners of fate, but prisoners of their own minds.

—FRANKLIN D. ROOSEVELT

World history is witness to many significant human achievements through sheer willpower and strong determination.

The mantra talks of good thoughts in the mind. Good thoughts that relate to happiness, welfare, friendship, respect and harmony generate positivity. Thought is one clear human action. Every action has an equal and opposite reaction. Every thought originating in the mind generates a set of vibrations which are, in common parlance, called vibes. These vibrations travel through the ethereal space and are received by those for whom they are meant. So, thoughts of love and friendship for someone will reach that person and influence him/her in a positive way. The reactionary thoughts in that person will generate positive vibes from him/her that will come back to the former person. A chain reaction of positive vibes and positivity is thereby set up. This chain reaction enhances peace. On the other hand, negative thoughts of hatred, anger or jealousy generate negative vibrations and create an atmosphere of mistrust, fear and gloom.

Thoughts are the seeds of activity. More than that, thoughts are the first actions committed. Other actions follow in accordance with the thoughts.

It is easy to see that in the present world, devious and evil thoughts are commonplace. Outward actions are positive and friendly to suit the occasion or purpose. There is dissonance between thought and action. Often the facial expressions of a person do not match his/her thoughts. There is also discrepancy in one's speech and action. This is deceit. This is dishonesty. This is devious demeanour.

A wandering mind is the dissipater of energy. A focussed mind uses that energy in the most productive and optimal way. You can increase your working efficiency manifold through better mental focus. Through mental training, it is possible to develop a photographic memory. Concentration is the key in this. This Vedic mantra tells you about the nature and one characteristic of the human mind. Other mantras in this sequence talk of other unique characteristics of the mind.

If you make any positive and noble resolve in your mind, it will settle in its backend portion called the subconscious. This subconscious portion is 90 per cent of the mind and is extremely powerful. It subtly and covertly influences the working of the conscious mind, which constitutes only 10 per cent of the mind. The subconscious is the seat of programming of the self, akin to the programming done in computer hardwares through softwares. The softwares then are the resolves as talked of above.

Whatever we plant in our subconscious mind and nourish with repetition and emotion will one day become a reality.
—EARL NIGHTINGALE

Human happiness is a measure of inner wellness—of inner peace and harmony. Inner wellness depends upon a state of inner satisfaction and inner fulfilment, a state of absence of frustration, discontent, fear, anger and jealousy. It also depends upon the absence of physical pain and discomfort. Therefore, sound physical and mental health creates inner wellness. Physical health is characterized by the absence of disease, while mental health is characterized by the absence of discontent, anger and sorrow. The mind has a great role in this. Therefore, it is through the instrument of the mind that inner wellness is to be realized.

This mantra of the Veda gives you the instrument with which to achieve mental focus and concentration, which form the foundation of high-quality work and success in all endeavours. At present we are utilizing only about 5 per cent of our mental and intellectual powers. But we can increase it to 7 per cent, 10 per cent and even more.

Chant this mantra for 20 minutes on a daily basis and see the effect on your mind. See the mind developing greater focus and concentration. See yourself become more perseverant. See yourself become more successful, wealthier. See yourself become more peaceful, less quarrelsome, less intemperate. The mantra comes not from the imperfect human, but from the perfect God, who is omniscient. Hence, it carries unmistakable potency and power. Mental focus is the virtual vehicle of victorious endeavours. The mind was given by the Creator. Only the Creator's advice as adumbrated in the Vedas can help us to use this wonderful instrument effectively and optimally. Human development hinges upon the functioning of this fantastic tool.

To master your mind is to master your life. Mental conditioning based on its noble resolve is the same as 'mind hacking', a term used by modern psychologists. Mind hacking involves three steps—analysing, imagining and reprogramming. While analysing the situation you are in, you have to fix your goal in a realistic manner. In that process, you have to consider the reality that you are not your mind. Imagination sets up the base for realizing the seemingly difficult or impossible goal. And reprogramming builds up the mental framework for creating the imagined thing. A good practical way to perform analysis and reprogramming is to write down your daily goals and achievements in your personal diary and see your efforts pouring in your idea. Through skill, iteration and persistence, we translate the idea into a reality.

TWENTY-ONE

Tame Your Mind: Set Righteous Thoughts in It

> *Aum yenakarmanyapaso manishino yajyekrinawanti vidathey shudheerah. Yadapurvam yakshamantah prajanaam tanmey manah shivasankalpamastu.*
>
> (O Lord! The erudite and the seers control their minds effectively, engage in yagyas and perform good deeds. This wonderful mind exists in every human being. May my mind be filled with good thoughts and noble resolves.)
> —YAJUR VEDA 34.2

The key to perseverance and success is mind control. The erudite people who are knowledgeable and learned by experience understand this fact better than ordinary ones. They engage in yagyas for their own upliftment and for the welfare of the larger community. The seers are enlightened individuals with vision for the future good of humanity. Such visionaries become the instruments of cataclysmic changes in the society. They are the ones who play a pivotal role in the ushering in of a new order and discarding the old one. But how are the above-mentioned learned people and seers different from the ordinary rut of humans? They are able to control their minds well.

Reality exists in the human mind, and nowhere else.
—GEORGE ORWELL, *1984*

There are two requisites for success and happiness; right knowledge and right action. Right action takes effect through mind control. One can see here the great importance of mind control. Without mind control, any amount of knowledge is useless simply because action has to take effect through the medium of the mind. And the mind is erratic, behaving like an unbridled horse. It disobeys you, conflicts with you and drags you into zones of negativity. The mind has to be brought under control because it is the commander of our senses. Without mind control, consistent right action by humans is not possible. The human is inherently weak. His/her knowledge and understanding are imperfect. He/she needs to exercise control over his/her mind not only to avoid indulgence in bad karmas but also to accumulate right knowledge and refine his/her understanding.

Next, this mantra talks of yagyas. The seers perform yagyas. Yagyas deliver benefits to the ecosystem, to other living beings including fellow men. Yagyas are participatory and collaborative activities for the welfare and upliftment of all participants.

The individual is expected to perform three different types of yagya on a daily basis. These are Brahma yagya, Deva yagya and Balivaishwadeva yagya. Brahma yagya comprises praise of, prayer to and meditation upon God. Deva yagya is the performance of fire oblations to nourish and purify the five basic elements of nature called panchabhut i.e. earth, water, fire, air and ether. Balivaishwadeva yagya refers to the act of feeding the lower animals and birds. There are two more types of yagya prescribed by the Vedas. These are Pitri yagya (oblations to the ancestors) and Atithi yagya (serving the learned visitors). The seers regularly perform all these yagyas. In addition, they are involved in preaching and spreading the divine message of the Vedas. This is also a yagya. The seers, being enlightened and saintly individuals, are the role models for the common folks in that they keep their minds under control, perform life-elevating yagyas and do virtuous deeds. They are worthy of emulation by the ordinary members of the society.

Thought in the mind is one action performed that will bring retributive effect. Good, positive and optimistic thoughts, and progressive ideas—all drive the mind at both conscious and subconscious levels. The subconscious mind develops tendencies to take the individual in such directions as are consistent with those thoughts. This is the power of positive thinking. Positive thoughts also emit positive vibrations into ethereal space. These vibrations originating from a person reach the subjects of his/her thoughts and influence those subjects into positive responses that are in the nature of similar vibrations returning to the person concerned. A chain response phenomenon is thereby created which, over a period of time, leads to realization of the objective contained in the original train of thoughts.

> *The biggest wall you have to climb is the one you build in your mind: Never let your mind talk you out of your dreams, trick you into giving up. Never let your mind become the greatest obstacle to success. Try to get your mind on the right track, the rest will follow.*
> —ROY T. BENNETT, *The Light in the Heart*

If you think that you are unable to overcome lassitude and lethargy even if you possess a clear goal, you need to chant this mantra on a daily basis. The latent power of the mantra will develop your willpower and help you to get the better of laziness, which is the worst enemy of progress. And do remember, a lazy person is an unhappy person. He gives in to negative thoughts easily because an idle mind is a devil's workshop. The mantra tells us the power of yagya to make us perseverant and virtuous. The ancient Aryans—natives of India—performed *agnihotra yagya* every day at dawn and dusk. The yagya works scientifically to refine the human intellect and strengthen human willpower. The way to success and happiness is through the mind. Make a determination to shed lethargy and procrastination. The potency of this mantra will be demonstrated through chanting and the miraculous effect of that.

Currently there is a lot of literature on stress alleviation. You find books by the hundreds on how to lead happier lives and how to gain success in your endeavours. There are numerous authors suggesting various approaches and philosophies in these books. Today, with the internet and the mobile telephone becoming universal tools of daily activities, every bit of information is just a click away. But has such a huge amount of information enabled mankind to become substantially more productive, efficient and happy? There is a yawning gap between theory and application of knowledge. The information itself needs to be in a clear, crisp and intelligible form. The internet provides loose and diffused information. People remain confused and are unable to apply such information for their benefit. The solution to this problem is prudence in the use of information which, in turn, means developing your intellectual strength. A good way of filtering and crystallizing useful information is writing down notes and preserving it for frequent reference.

Very often, people find themselves unable to hold together their minds and intellects. The intellect understands things, but the mind disobeys it. Therefore, as aforesaid, use the tremendous divine power of this mantra through chanting to increase your willpower, enabling you to absorb and apply truthful and factual information from the sea of loose strands of information available. Based on this, you will be able to rein in your errant mind and qualitatively improve your karmas. You will be able to truly transform your lives.

TWENTY-TWO

The Basis of Intelligence, Memory and Knowledge

Aum yatpragyan mutachaito
dhritishchayajjyotirantaramritam prajasu.
Yasmaanritey kinchan karma kriyatey, tanmey manah
shivasankalpam astu.

(The mind is the source of intelligence, memory and knowledge and nothing can be achieved without its help. May my mind be filled with noble ambitions and determinations)

—YAJUR VEDA 34.3

The mind is the source of intelligence. But what is intelligence?

The human soul picks up threads of knowledge from the outside world. It hears through the ears, sees through the eyes and smells through the nose. Without mind at the back, these activities of perception are not possible. The mind being the controller of senses, directs them at the objects of perception. After that comes the role of the intellect that enables the soul to understand, decipher, analyse and classify the perception signal. So without mind, the perceptive activity could never take place. Intelligence is the ability to decipher information gathered through sensory perception and this intelligence cannot be called into play without the action of the mind. Hence, the mind is the source of intelligence.

The mind is also the source of memory. Memory is the storage of deciphered information. Raw information, after it is understood by the intellect, is transferred to the subconscious portion of the mind. It is a huge storehouse of information, well comparable with a microcomputer.

The mind then is also the indirect source of all knowledge because all knowledge is due to human consciousness and the mind is the epicentre of consciousness.

In view of the above, it is only obvious that nothing in human life is achievable without the help of the mind. The mind is the fulcrum of all human activities. The mind has to be regulated and refined to create a train of right thoughts that will take us to our individual goals.

We are shaped by our thoughts; we become what we think. When the mind is pure, joy follows like a shadow that never leaves.

—BUDDHA

Stress is a state when we are gripped by worry, anxiety or fear. These states are attributable to the mind. Worry, anxiety and fear are states that are caused by a wandering mind. A lazy person who whiles away time has an idle mind and an idle mind is a devil's workshop. It is the breeding ground of worry that is futile. Fear is a condition caused by the lack of knowledge and understanding. Fear is also due to moral transgression or due to such actions that are unrighteous. Actions that do not carry sanction of the society and community generate fear. Hence, alleviation of stress is a matter of mind management. Keeping yourself busy in meaningful and productive activities is the best antidote to stress that can be.

When the mind is the source of intelligence, memory and knowledge, mind management will necessitate honing of intelligence, sharpening of memory and refinement of knowledge. Meditation, intake of sattvic (pure, fresh vegetarian) food, pranayam (breath control), brahmacharya (sexual continence) and prayer to God are ways to improve your memory and intelligence.

The Gayatri Mantra of the Vedas contains prayer to the Almighty for refinement of intelligence and understanding. Regular chanting of the Gayatri Mantra enables you to understand people and things better. Good relationships with people hinge upon understanding of their attitudes, intentions and perspectives. These days, relationship issues constitute the biggest cause of stress in daily life. Relations with the peer, with the spouse, with the workplace superior, with the business partner—all are under strain and generate stress. In these stressful relationships, it is mostly the lack of proper understanding of the other person's perspective that generates misunderstanding, anger and irritation.

We also do need to understand that our expectations from others are always high. But what about the expectations from our own selves? The latter need to be high, really. We can do much more for relationship improvement by enhanced expectation from our own selves than by any other approach.

Refinement of knowledge is the other term for better understanding. Better understanding comes when you shed anger, as mentioned above. Better understanding of others and situations also comes when you shed arrogance and develop humility.

Stress in the modern professional and corporate world is often because of performance gaps. Where these performance gaps are due to lower functional efficiency, there comes the role of such interventional tools as this Vedic mantra.

The human organism is a very complex entity. To understand this complex entity, the human being needs to use the knowledge and perspective of the creator of human beings whose messages and injunctions to his subjects are enshrined in the Vedic texts. This is so because our Creator knows us best. We humans are intellectually imperfect; we are incapable of understanding ourselves completely and comprehensively. It, therefore, makes perfect sense to take guidance from the Vedas for resolution of all our problems.

Since this mantra emphasizes on the fact that the mind is the essential contrivance for the performance of any task, it is the key factor in performance efficiency. Chanting of this mantra on a regular basis will enhance your working efficiency. These days, much literature is available on the subject of professional productivity enhancement. Books by the dozen provide formatted plans to corporate managers for improving employee and labour productivity. But there is a mantra angle to it also. This mantra works through divine medium and shows its effect in unmistakable terms. It provides clarity of thought to the practitioner, improves information retention and comprehension of facts, which are often shrouded under layers of misinformation and false propaganda.

Knowledge is power and knowledge is acquired through the working of the mind, but the mind itself is a product of programming. And behind this programming is the power of imagination.

Imagination is more powerful than knowledge.
—ALBERT EINSTEIN

Imagination sets the mind and programmes it in the positive direction which takes you unquestionably to your charted goal. It is the soft power of your subconscious mind that drives the conscious mind in the right direction. This imagination is exactly the resolve talked of in this divine Vedic mantra.

Chant this mantra of the Vedas daily for 15 minutes and see its effect on your mind. The preferred time of chanting of this mantra is the evening time, around sunset and alternatively before retiring to bed. See and experience the progressive effect of this chanting on your mind. See your intelligence, memory and understanding power sharpen incrementally over time. See you mental strength improving with each session. With improvement of your mental strength, positive thoughts will begin to settle in your mental space and negativities of all kinds will diminish. You will begin to harbour noble ambitions with a strong resolve to realize those ambitions. After all, all humans desire happiness and success. Mind is the tool which most frequently lets them down. Rein in the errant mind by tapping the divine power locked in this mantra. The word 'mantra' literally means a tool for shaping of the mind. You can shape your mind in the positive and progressive way by using this divine device.

TWENTY-THREE

The Prime Tool of Yogic Practice

Aum yenedam bhutam bhuvanam bhavishyata parigrihi tamamritenasarvam. Yenayagyastayatey saptahota tanmey manah shivasankalpam astu.

(This mind, connected with the immortal creator God holds the key to understanding the past, the present and the future. This mind controls the seven karmic sense organs and is the prime instrument of the performance of yagyas. May this mind be full of noble resolves.)

—YAJUR VEDA 34.4

The mind, the intellect and the ego self of a human being are subtle entities, but the supersoul God is the most subtle substance and, therefore, contains everything including the wonderful human mind within it. When the mind is focussed on its creator God, it is said to be connected with it. God is omniscient. He possesses complete knowledge of the past and the present and of possibilities in the future. The mind is actually an appendage of the human soul. Through this appendage, the soul operates the various sense organs of the human body. Like the mind, the soul is also contained in God. When the soul sets itself into yogic communion with God, there occurs an automatic and concurrent connection of the mind with Him. When the mind is connected with God in this manner, it gives to the soul multidimensional vision and clairvoyance. The soul thereby acquires the power of vision of the past and a discriminatory, sharp judgment of the present. It also acquires a directional vision of the future. In this Vedic mantra, the attributes and role of the human mind have been further explained.

The past, present and future are actually for us, not for the creator God who is eternally in the present. He is beyond time. The concept of time is for us humans who are witness to day, night and the cyclic seasons. The concept of time is also limited to the realm of our solar system and subject to the theory of relativity, which relates time to the speed of light through which humans perceive events in time. If we go outside our solar system, the concept of time remains but time acquires a different dimension. If we travel faster than the speed of light, time acquires an entirely different concept. This mantra of the Veda tells you that the mind is the key factor in the perception of time by humans. Definitely, because the mind is the instrument of all perceptions.

The past is understood through the stored memories in the subconscious portion of the mind. The past is also visualized by those accomplished in the practice of yoga. All past events remain in the ethereal space in a coded form and these can be decoded through yoga. The present is visible and perceptible by all ordinary humans, but those who practise yoga can observe existential reality more closely, accurately and effectively. The present is the most important time. It is the time of action which will fashion the future in the desired manner. It is the time for improvement, refinement and upgradation of character by learning from the past. The past has no material value otherwise. It's only value, therefore, is as a reference for the present and the future. We do not have to dwell in the past or brood over the past events and waste time of the present. The mind has to be trained accordingly. Training of the mind and mind control hold the key to successful accomplishment of all tasks—small or gigantic.

Don't limit yourself. Many people limit themselves to what they think they can do. You can go as far as your mind lets you. What you believe, remember, you can achieve.
—MARY KAY ASH

The past is an expired cheque, the future a post-dated cheque and the present is a present—a ready gift. Let us train the mind to make use of this gift to shape our lives for realizing our noble ambitions. This Vedic mantra brings us this lesson.

The focal point in all the above is again the mind. But training of the mind is an ordeal. It is easier said than done. The mind is so fickle, so wavering, so errant. Practise of yoga is the key to mind control.

But mind control largely deals with the conscious mind, which is 10 per cent portion of the mind. What about the other 90 per cent called the subconscious mind, which covertly exercises influence on the conscious mind and powerfully? The subconscious mind is a huge storehouse of information and impressions, often carried over from distant past spanning hundreds and thousands of years which cover many past lives of the person.

And what of the future? The future is indeterminable. Trends and possibilities of events in the future are determinable though. The creator God who is omniscient knows the past karmas of a person and also knows the time spans in which those karmas will fructify. To that extent, He knows the destiny of a person and the events that are precipitated by the forces of destiny. The absolute future is entirely indeterminable. Because not only man but even his creator does not know what karmas will be performed by someone in the future. A person is entirely free in the performance of his/her karmas—qualitatively and quantitatively. God does not interfere in this performance. And all karmas will bear qualitative fruits according to the immanent law of cause and effect.

Our mind enables us to understand the law of karmic retribution and the importance of good, life-elevating karmas. Not only that, the power-packed instrument called mind also coveys to such a person what kind of results he/she can expect from his/her karmas. What he/she does not know is when in time a particular karma will fructify. That is best known only to the Creator as explained above and for the right reasons.

You have to perform a yagya for deriving benefits in any area or walk of life. A student works hard to complete his academic coursework with distinction. An athlete performs untiring regular practice to come good and give a medal-winning performance at the next Olympics. A businessperson in the field of manufacturing invests more money in new factories and employs more professionals to upscale his/her business. A wealthy person liberally performs philanthropy and donates for charity to help the deprived and the downtrodden. All these are examples of yagya where an individual does some activity for the welfare of others and, in turn, helps himself/herself by deriving material benefits or otherwise by accumulating good fortune.

The human mind is the focal agent in the performance of all the above yagyas.

This Vedic mantra carries the potency of refining human karma. It aligns the mind with truth by helping a person to learn from his/her past experiences and with a clear progressive vision for the future, enables the person to make the best use of the present time. Chanting of this mantra on a regular basis makes this happen. Let the readers practise and experience it for themselves.

Take any noble resolve depending upon your individual desires and aspirations. Set a target or an achievement milestone to reach and firmly fix it in your mind. Visualize yourself achieving that target. Speak out loud five times, in the morning and in the evening, that you will achieve that target. This will align your conscious mind and, more importantly, the subconscious mind with your goal and the latter will start working in that direction. Modern psychologists have discovered the concept of mind reprogramming and developed techniques to alter the mental software. The basic element in this technique is repeated resolve—in writing or orally or mentally—for realization of positive states and positive goals of the individual. This shows in definite terms the great scientific truth contained in the Vedic mantras.

The outside world will cooperate with it in this process and the goal will be realized in due course of time. This is the power of mental determination. It alters the software of the subconscious mind to drive the individual towards his goal. This book is about inner wellness and inner wellness depends upon the realization of inner desires and the fulfilment of inner aspirations, apart from other factors. The importance of this mantra and its application cannot be overemphasized in this context. Regular practice of this mantra, which includes chanting, is bound to give a person a better and clearer understanding of the past and present and a clearer perspective on the possibilities in the future. That will equip him/her powerfully to fulfill his/her aspirations.

TWENTY-FOUR

The Key Instrument of Knowledge Acquisition

Aum yasminricha samayajugwamshi yasminpratishthita rathnabhavivara. Yasmins chitagwam sarvamotam prajanaam tanmey manah shivasankalpam astu.

(The mind in which the Rig Veda, Yajur Veda and Sama Veda are embedded like the spokes of a chariot wheel and in which all knowledge of living creatures is arranged like pearls threaded together—may that mind harbour noble thoughts and be devoted to noble causes.)

—YAJUR VEDA 34.5

The mind is the storehouse of all information and knowledge. As explained in the previous mantra, the subconscious portion of the mind is the memory storage space. After the onset of creation, when the first humans appeared on earth, it was necessary to impart them the knowledge of all types, so that they could perform actions to refine themselves and grow spiritually, thus fulfilling the objective of human birth. God published the four Vedas—the Rig Veda, the Yajur Veda, the Sama Veda and the Atharva Veda—in the minds of four seers Agni, Vayu, Aditya and Angira respectively. These four seers were pure, enlightened souls and had perfect, photographic memories.

The knowledge enshrined in the Vedas was passed on to successive generations through oral transmission.

This Vedic mantra tells categorically that all knowledge of living beings is contained in the Vedas and it is the human mind which is the physical storage space of this knowledge.

The Rig Veda is the text of all fundamental, core knowledge. It contains the prime principles and precepts of all knowledge. It forms the foundation of healthcare, mind control, trade and business, politics and statecraft, spirituality, jurisprudence and all other worldly subjects. It is the Veda to refer to when confronted with a situation attended by wide dissonance of thoughts and absence of clarity and consensus. The precepts provided in the Rig Veda are clear and universalistic and help in bringing the required consensus among people who zealously or arrogantly cling on to their individual opinions. The human mind plays the pivotal part in the performance of the above actions.

The Yajur Veda is the Veda of action. It provides direction to the human being for right action, guidance for the appropriate karma in all situations. Its injunctions tell a person to overcome his/her deficiencies and overpower his/her enemies, both internal and external. It explains to him/her the benefits of yagya and the power of perseverance. It exhorts him/her to disseminate true knowledge and its application techniques. It tells him/her the right ways of administering people, it teaches one to be fearless in the discharge of his/her noble duties. It enjoins upon him/her to maintain friendly relations with others. It exhorts him/her to absorb all true knowledge from the Vedas and use it to work for the welfare and upliftment of others. The above actions are all performed through the mind.

The Sama Veda is the Veda of devotion. Its mantras convey to a person to stay connected to the creator God through meditative communion. It emphasizes upon the importance of faith, upon the enormous power of faith to uplift man. The mantras of the Sama Veda provide balm for a stressed person. They help to alleviate tension and fear. The connection with the almighty God helps a person to achieve inner harmony and inner wellness. The divine happiness and joy derived out of devotional connection with God quells a person's inner confusion, worry and fear. Benefits of chanting the Sama Veda mantras and of performing meditation on God in accordance with them accrue to a person through the mind. The mind is central to the existence of man. Its conditioning helps one to overcome sorrow and attain happiness.

This mantra of the Yajur Veda reveals to a person the secret of the power of mind to make use of the divine knowledge laid down in the Vedas for happiness, success and progress. In his/her mind, the person must make the specific positive determination to realize a goal in order to actually reach that goal. The mind is the tapping ladle for the divine nectar that flows from the supersoul God pervading the infinite universe and beyond it.

The book *The Secret* authored by Rhonda Byrne became a global bestseller. The reason? The book describes the power of mind and the power of positive thinking and positive determination. The philosophy underlying this comes from this mantra of the Vedas.

Make any positive, noble determination in your mind—determination to achieve a goal. This goal may be for an undergraduate student aiming for an A grade in academic coursework, the captain of the national soccer team aspiring for the next World Cup, police commissioner of a city to reduce crime rate by 50 per cent in two years, the CEO of a corporate house getting set to double his/her business turnover in the next three years, a spiritually inclined person to attain salvation or an obese youngster wanting to shed half his weight in six months.

> *Here is an easy way to become a genius: give your subconscious mind strong 'why' and 'what', and it comes back with an amazing 'how' in due course.*
> —VADIM KOTELNIKOV

Every morning and evening, speak out aloud asserting and affirming your determined achievement of that particular goal. And then slowly and inexorably see your mind start working in that direction—both overtly and covertly. In due course of time, you will see that goal come true. But goals are not realized through some magical process. The process is scientific. The process involves right knowledge and its correct application. The right knowledge as also the right techniques will be revealed to you through interaction with the more experienced folks and self-discourse of the divine Vedic texts. And application is perseverance which means well-directed and consistent efforts.

The mind programmed through positive determination will ensure that the above happens, systematically.

As mentioned in the foregoing lines, the subconscious part of our mind is our software centre. Determination is the software that gets embedded in the mind. That software works its way forward in time to realize its coded goal. How does it happen? It works through the human astral body to attract the forces in the universe that facilitate the realization of the goal. But, to maintain peace, the person should not harbour a material goal that can only be realized through some violation of the tenets of dharma. It could be in the nature of a yagya defined in the Vedas as a collaborative activity bringing benefits to all and harm to none.

The powers of the subconscious mind are truly enormous. Great feats in life can be achieved by harnessing these powers. This is a wonderful secret that is not shared by many people. But the bigger secret is that the power of the mind is actually the power of the soul and, more than that, the power of the supersoul God. This is a scientific fact and in accordance with this facet of spiritual science, we should be working our way to success and happiness.

TWENTY-FIVE

Noble Thoughts for the Restive and Ageless Mind

> *Aum susharathirashwaniva yanmanushyanney niyatey abhishubhirwa jinaiva. Hratpratishtham yadajiram javishtham tanmey manah shivasankalpam astu.*
>
> (A proficient charioteer keeps the strong and restless horses of the chariot in control. In a similar way, may we control our mind which takes us here and there with great rapidity in the jungle of thoughts. May that ageless mind, which is situated in the heart, be filled with good thoughts and noble resolves.)
>
> —YAJUR VEDA 34.6

The Katha Upanishad says:

> The human being is similar to a chariot pulled by horses. The body of the chariot is the human physical body; the horses steering the chariot are the human senses. Human mind is the bridle of all these horses. The charioteer who holds the bridle is the human intellect and the traveller who is seated in the chariot is the human soul.

The above is a perfect metaphorical expression for anyone who wishes to understand true human nature and the importance of the mind. The mind is erratic and tends to go wayward. The fools drift with it or follow it, while the wise control it. A polluted mind is the passport to hell and a pure mind is the contrivance for success and happiness. Each one of us should keep the mind under control.

We are continually witness to the play of the mind and the intellect. The wayward mind is so strong that instead of being controlled by the intellect, it starts influencing it. The intellect loses its grip on the mind and then the mind starts ruling and leading the individual. It can take one to the territory of peace, contentment and happiness and it can also lead one into marshy soils of sorrow and wretchedness. It all depends on the influences that the mind is subjected to from time to time. It depends on the long-lasting impressions created on the mind. Therefore, the mind must be imparted good influences. It should be given good and healthy impressions. It should harbour noble thoughts. It should be programmed properly for progress, success, happiness and salvation.

Imagination rules the world—says an English proverb. You eventually become what you repeatedly imagine in your mind. Your thoughts and imaginations continuously shape and reshape the programming software in your subconscious mind. But does the mind always obey you? Does it follow every instruction of yours? Does it behave like a faithful servant? The mind is very erratic and excitable.

> *My mind is like my web browser. 19 tabs are open, 3 are frozen and I have no idea where the music is coming from.*
>
> —ANONYMOUS

The mind makes you err. The mind makes you procrastinate. The mind makes you sin. The mind makes you eat the forbidden fruit. We talk of mental fix; we talk of mental aberration.

All the above statements corroborate what this Vedic mantra says. The mantra also calls the human mind ageless. The material things that we see around us are all subject to ageing. They degrade and deteriorate with time. The human and animal body ages and lasts a predetermined time span. The human mind is also material in constitution, but it does not age. It is not immortal nor is it static or unchanging. It undergoes changes and transformation over time, but it does not die till the time of dissolution of the universe created by God. The mind comes into existence at the onset of creation when it is given to the eternal soul. Thereafter it remains attached to the immortal soul as an appendage till the time of dissolution of the universe. Hence, it is not immortal like the soul, but it is ageless. It does not deteriorate and die. It keeps on changing its characteristics and colours.

Good thoughts and noble ambitions are the programming software of a person's mind to make him positive, productive, peaceful and pious. Today's generation revels in its scientific achievements. Information technology has brought more automation and robotics is the in thing today. We saw the age of computers dawn on us. It was only a few decades back. This was quickly and quite inexorably followed by the emergence of the internet and now more changes and technological breakthroughs are on the horizon. Nanotechnology has given us the power to alter the structure of the gene at will and create clones of animals, plants and humans.

But we still know little about the human mind. It will take a much longer time for the intelligent humans to understand the intricacies of the mind. But why not take a cue from the messages of the Vedas and try to use the mind for our greater benefits? This mantra contains exactly that subtle wisdom and fine message. We can bring about big and extensive changes in the world through engineering of the mind.

If you can't change the world, change your mind.
—ANONYMOUS

Chant this mantra on a daily basis and see its magical effect on your mind. You are floating in an infinite sea of spirituality. This sea of spirituality is the creator God. The mind is the subtle tool to tap this sea. The spiritual substance called God has the power to purge our mind of all negatives. This spiritual substance is the antidote to fear, illusion and sorrow. It has the power to annihilate worry, despair and gloom. It is the harbinger of hope. The creator is the true father, mother, brother, sister and friend of a person. He is the teacher, preceptor and guide. The mind is the ultimate tool available with the human being to tap the beneficence of the Creator. It is a unique entity—like the unique creator and the unique you, the immortal and eternal soul.

Chanting of this mantra will also enable a person to focus and concentrate better. What is more important and crucial for success than focus and concentration? Nothing, absolutely. Concentration pours in all your energy in the task at hand and makes optimal use of your faculties in its performance. It is the key to efficiency and optimization. Computer hardware, software, management techniques and systems and organization behaviour practices are but of secondary importance in this regard. Mental focus is of primary importance. It is akin to the case when you concentrate the rays of the sun through a convex lens on a piece of paper and the spot where sunlight is focussed begins to burn. These days, there is a lot of glib talk on multitasking.

Multitasking actually dissipates mental focus and results in the decline of working efficiency. And multitasking considered in conjunction with the digital technology tools such as iPhones and apps takes a greater toll on this efficiency. Our mind is inherently like the mischievous monkey in the backyard but with such gizmos in our hand, it behaves like a squirrel in our front yard.

This mantra has the inherent power to calm down and rein in the excitable mind.

Besides the above, the divine power contained in this mantra enables you to do a very important thing to help yourself navigate successfully through this jungle of life. And that is self-control, as it is with some of the previous mantras. Self-control is the master key to correct all wrongs, to set right every situation and matter in your outright favour. It is the best contrivance to smother the other person's anger and arrogance. It is the divinely given technique with which to act smart, act wise and act complete. It is verily the most effective tool to realize your own enormous potential in this precious life.

The human soul is an indestructible entity with consciousness and intelligence. There is a huge, almost infinite amount of energy in this vast universe, only to be tapped and used constructively and beneficially. The conscious soul can do it, coupled with right knowledge. The Creator is always there to help, guide and facilitate things. He wants you to fulfil your dreams and reach your goals. He is an infinite storehouse of all knowledge, intelligence and power. Unflinching faith in Him with mental resolve will make everything good happen for you.

Regular chanting of this mantra brings exactly the results prayed for. It enables our intellect to gain better control over the mind, thus opening us to the great possibilities of charting our own desired course in life. It will make us powerful and focussed to carve out our own destiny—in the manner we want to become, fulfilling our deep desires and aspirations all the way. It is another drop from the infinite ocean of beneficence and bliss that the creator God is. Let us go ahead and tap something from that ocean. We can do it in this one life and do not worry—we can do it in the next life or lives also if we fail to do it in this life. God is compassionate and gives you multiple chances and many opportunities. He is your true friend, philosopher and guide because besides being compassionate, He is also omniscient. You will receive perfect guidance from Him. And don't forget, He is an infinite pool of beneficence as mentioned above. You can get what you desire through Him. You have to have resolute faith in Him and proceed forward.

TWENTY-SIX

Health and Happiness from Meditation on God

Aum sanapawaswa shangavey sham janaey shamarvatey; sham rajannaushadhibhyah.

(When the devotee meditates on God, peace comes to his cognitive senses making them regulated; peace comes to his genital sensory organ, making him sexually disciplined: peace comes to his mind bringing him composure and peace comes in his body internals, freeing him of disease.)

—SAMA VEDA 1.3

This mantra of the Sama Veda has a big message to convey. It tells the Creator's human subject that his/her meditative activity on God brings him/her multifold benefits. The multiple meanings of peace are brought out tersely in this divine mantra. The entire Sama Veda is centred on bhakti, or devotion. It is the Veda of devotion to the creator God.

Devotion to an entity means a total sense of respect and surrender with a desire to appease that entity. A majority of the hymns contained in the Sama Veda deal with meditative communion with God. They convey that divine nectar flows to us when we connect ourselves with our Creator through such technique. This divine nectar flowing from the supreme spiritual substance God has the power to purge us of our mental negativities, refine our sensory organs and even free us of physical ailments. The wonderful thing is to understand how all this happens scientifically.

As discussed earlier, the five cognitive senses are sight, hearing, smell, taste and touch. Peace means calmness, stability and purity. All these external sensory organs dealing with cognition—the eyes, ears, nose, tongue and the skin—become healthier and the corresponding sensory faculties grow sharper. Why? God as the most subtle substance holds supreme power. It, therefore, exercises complete control over all matter. This control is exercised from within outwards, in a centrifugal mode because the God substance is subtler than atoms and even subtler than their constituent particles—electrons, protons, neutrons and positrons. The human body is made up of these particles, like any other material object.

Next, this mantra talks of peace coming to the genital sense organs. Peace to these organs connotes sexual discipline coming to a person. Sexual discipline is extremely important. Sexual activity dissipates a huge amount of one's internal vital energy called ojas. This ojas is the element that gives strength, stamina, endurance and vitality to the body. It promotes longevity. That is why it is important to preserve this element. Sexual activity dissipates this element and sexual continence preserves it. Sexual profligacy destroys a person.

Meditative communion with God makes a person's thoughts purer. It weans him/her away from objects of desire and sexual stimulation. It weans them from a repetitive desire for sexual gratification. Desire for sexual gratification takes root in the human mind. And as discussed in the earlier chapters, thoughts in the mind constitute action, which carries a trail of reactions as well as a retributive effect. So regulation of amorous thoughts originating in the mind means nipping the evil in the bud.

This mantra thereafter says that meditation upon God brings mental peace. This is one big answer to the question posed by modern life—the question of how to overcome stress. Stress is a widespread malady afflicting the young, middle aged and the old alike. This book is also about stress alleviation. Inner wellness is all about overcoming inner stress. Meditative communion with God provides the golden key to stress reduction. God, being the infinite live reservoir of positivity and omnipotent and compassionate at the same time, kindles hope and generates a sense of security. The divine nectar flowing from Him to His human subject during meditation thus reduces or removes the latter's worry, fear and remorse.

> *Meditation is not evasion; it is a serene encounter with reality.*
>
> —THICH NHAT HANH

Get up early in the morning, about two hours before sunrise. That is the best time to perform meditation upon the creator God. Sit cross-legged with the spine and head erect. In this posture, take a long breath in and then slowly exhale out the air. After exhaling, hold your breath. Hold it for as long as you can. Release your breath and revert to normal breathing pattern. Then, with eyes closed, try to clear your mind of all stray and fleeting thoughts. This is not easy. But it comes with practice. If fleeting thoughts enter your mind despite your efforts to clear them, try to remove them by inner chanting of the syllable Aum, the original and fundamental name of the creator God. This way you will be able to achieve a mental state of zero thoughts. Remain in this condition for five minutes. Then, mentally inscribe the syllable 'Aum' on your forehead and concentrate upon it. Do it for two minutes. Then, for three minutes think about the attributes of the Creator that you know. Complete this 10-minute activity. Do it for a few days and see the results. Continue doing it for three weeks and it will become a habit. Do not give up this habit. Your life will be transformed.

> *He [Buddha] spent six years meditating on the essence, causes, and cures for human anguish. In the end, he came to the realization that suffering is not caused by ill fortune, by social injustice, or by divine whims. Rather, suffering is caused by the behaviour patterns of one's mind.*
>
> —YUVAL NOAH HARARI, *SAPIENS*

Following the message conveyed by this mantra also generates positive vibrations which serve to correct the imbalance of vata, pitta and kapha—the three basic functional humours in the human body—and restore to health the body organs. The divine energy of the creator God, which fills the entire ethereal space, plays its part in this. 'Peace' as a term with a larger canvas of meaning also includes balance. Disease in the human body is caused by the imbalance of vata, pitta and kapha.

The creator God as the most subtle spiritual substance filling the entire space has complete control over all atoms and molecules. And the three functional humours stated above are only products of matter, made of atoms and molecules. Practising meditative communion with God as per the message of this mantra will give us multiple benefits. It is a mantra from the Sama Veda and hence devotional in essence. This mantra actually brings out the scientific nature of human interaction with God.

As mentioned earlier, during meditative communion with God, a divine nectar flows from the more subtle spiritual substance God to the less-subtle spirit called the human soul. From the soul, this divine nectar flows to its appendages—the conscious mind, the intellect, the subconscious mind and the ego self. It purifies all of them. The mind and the subconscious mind have control over all body organs. Purification of the mind results in purification of the body organs. Purification of the intellect makes it sharp and discriminative. Purification of the subconscious mind creates noble impressions in it and programmes it positively. Purification of the ego self makes the person humbler and more realistic. This is all-round improvement.

Meditation upon God is the technique of tapping that immortalizing nectar which has the power of freeing us from pain—both physical and mental. It is a great de-stressing approach. It is the way to the fulfilment of desire and liberation from sorrow. This great secret is revealed by this Vedic mantra. It is up to us to derive benefit out of it or to ignore it with scepticism. The choice is entirely ours.

TWENTY-SEVEN

Vibes of Fearlessness from Ether and Earth

Aum abhayam nah karatyantariksham abhayam dyavaprithivi ubheyimey. Abhayam pashchadabhayam purastadutaradadharadabhayam no astu.

(Aum! O Lord, may the celestial space ether and the earth make us fearless. May we not get fear from anywhere—front, behind, above or below.)

—ATHARVA VEDA 19.15.5

This Vedic mantra is the first mantra for acquiring fearlessness. The mantra contains prayer to the Almighty for banishing fear from the mind.

Fear is the state of the mind caused by ignorance and untruth. It is also the mental state resulting from disharmony and conflict.

Ignorance is the parent of fear.

—HERMAN MELVILLE

A toddler is afraid to move out of its mother's lap to that of an unknown person. He fears insecurity. Because he is ignorant whether the other person who sweetly entreats him is his friend or foe. You are afraid to trudge through a thick jungle at night, as there may be wild animals lurking around. A young boy who has just learnt driving is afraid to take his car to a crowded road for fear of losing control in the thick traffic. A schoolboy who has just quarrelled with his playmates is afraid to meet them the next day for fear of reprisal. A traffic law violator is afraid of the traffic policeman. An income tax offender is afraid of the income tax sleuths. An inefficient employee is afraid to face his superior at work. In the jungle, the weak fears the strong; so is the case in a regime bereft of law. Every living being fears death. In all the above examples, the element of fear is present. Fear is a feeling of impending danger or warning from a potential threat. It is the mental state in a situation of perceived risk. The danger may be physical. The risk may be risk to life, to the purse, to property or to health and well-being. But closely analysed, fear is a state of mind resulting from ignorance and illusion. When you are armed with facts pertaining to a situation and the knowledge of the right course of action, you can always take an optimal corrective action to minimize your loss or damage.

> *Nothing in life is to be feared, it is only to be understood. Now is the time to understand more, so that we may fear less.*
>
> —MARIE CURIE

In the modern business world, entrepreneurs are aware of all the potential risks that launching a new business venture entails. Even while taking calculated risks, they have a lurking fear in their minds—the fear of failure. The fear of failure is rampant in the complex human life of the twenty-first century. Closely analysed and summarized, fear is the result of either the ignorance of the reality leading to uncertain situation or apprehension of reprisal by the enemy or dread of failure in task being undertaken. Fear emanates generally from uncertainties and imponderables.

The present mantra from the Atharva Veda prays for no fear from the sky, ether and earth and no fear emanating from any of the four planar directions (top, bottom, front and back). This situation can be realized only if we are knowledgeable about how we humans have handled the ether and earth elements, if we know the repercussions of mishandling done, if any. Today, our scientists including geography and meteorology experts claim to know a lot but are incapable of accurately predicting earthquakes, volcanic eruptions, landslides and tsunamis that bring harm or disaster to humans. We need to be equipped with knowledge—and true knowledge, not wallowing in illusion. And this is possible only if we are scientific and logical in our approach and in sync with the principles and precepts prescribed in the primeval scriptures, the Vedas. The Vedas contain all knowledge of the world and the universe in cryptic and coded form. With this faith and conviction at the back of our minds, we need to do extensive research and unravel the mysteries of Mother Nature. We need to know nature well and handle it well too.

> *Fear is the main source of superstition, and one of the main sources of cruelty. To conquer fear is the beginning of wisdom.*
>
> —BERTRAND RUSSELL

Chanting of this mantra on a regular basis assuages our fear from material things and harm-bringing living beings such as wild animals, insects and poisonous snakes from the outer environment. Many people suffer from schizophrenia, hallucinations, claustrophobia, hydrophobia and other types of conditions that have, inter alia, imaginary fears that often grip them. This mantra is a powerful remedy for such conditions as well. The working of the mantra takes place at the spiritual and psychic planes. It is scientific and in accordance with the eternal principles set in by the all-knowing creator. Freedom from fear is a big thing. Fear saps the energy as well as the vitality of a person. Since humans are inherently of limited intellectual capacity, he/she can never be in the full knowledge of things. Therefore, he/she has to regulate his/her life on a day-to-day and hour-to-hour basis to get the better of fear. One has to maintain physical fitness through a proper diet, exercise and adequate sleep. One also needs to have abiding faith in God and maintain everyday connection with Him through prayer and meditation. These will do a lot to help one overcome fear.

The four sides mentioned in this mantra refer to the entire space since these sides—top, bottom, front and rear—cover comprehensively the entire three-dimensional space. The negative vibrations of fear are experienced in the mind, no doubt about that. But the source and seeds of these vibrations are external objects and external entities—living or non-living. Therefore, the divine potency of this mantra quells the imaginary ideas related to these entities dispersed and distributed in the three-dimensional space covered by the abovesaid four directions.

Absence of fear gives a healthy and positive perspective to the mind. It makes the thinking clear and rational. It makes the person use his/her sensory organs and faculties intelligently, purposefully and smartly. It makes him/her victorious because victory lies in the zone of fearlessness. As said above, the usage of this mantra helps a person to overcome everyday fears of life. But it is also a potent instrument of spiritual healing. All mental ailments associated with fear of some type or the other are amenable to treatment through chanting of this mantra.

There is no inner wellness if there be fear present. Fear destroys mental peace as also sets in a morbid process in the physical body. It is the greatest obstacle in success because success in human endeavours requires calculated risk-taking. No one can take such risks without getting the better of fear. This mantra handed down by the Creator aids in exactly that.

Practise this mantra on a daily basis to experience a sense of inner security and fearlessness never experienced before. Remember, it is the voice and word of the creator God who knows all about your mind and body and intellect. You don't know many things about them, but He knows all. Hence, trust Him and have unwavering faith in Him. The world today suffers more because of the lack of faith or diminished faith than anything else. This mantra has the power to open up your inner front to the experience of boundless happiness and joy.

TWENTY-EIGHT

Freedom from All Fear: Day and Night

Aum abhayam mitradabhayam amitradabhayam gyatadabhayam parokshat. Abhayam naktamabhayam diva nah sarva asha mama mitram bhavantu.

(O God! May we have no fear of our friends or of our enemies. May we have no fear of known and unknown objects. May we have no fear of the day or the night. May the four planar directions protect us and provide us peace.)
—ATHARVA VEDA 19.15.6

This mantra is another gem out of the treasure trove of the Vedas. It talks of no fear from friends or from enemies. One can understand that there should be no fear of enemies but one is at a loss to understand the term 'fear of the friends'. Fear of the friend occurs when you harbour unkindly feelings towards your friend in the mind, howsoever transient or temporary they may be. In worldly situations, it occasionally happens that you have pangs of envy or jealousy in your minds even against your good friends, but you do not give outward expressions to them. More importantly, fear of the friend occurs when you are doing certain wrong actions that your friend strongly disapproves of.

Imagine a scenario: you are a chain-smoker and because of this vicious habit, you have developed chronic lung disease called bronchitis. Your friend, being your well-wisher, wants you to quit smoking. But you are unable to give up the habit completely. You give in to the compulsive urge to smoke frequently. If you have smoked a cigarette and your good friend calls on you, what will you feel? Fear, definitely.

The mantra of the Veda under explanation will make you boldly own your wrong action and you will not be afraid to hear the truth from your near and dear ones about the indiscretion that you have committed. You will become more honest and conscientious through the practce of this divine mantra.

One of the greatest discoveries a man makes, one of his great surprises, is to find he can do what he was afraid he couldn't do.

—HENRY FORD

Fear of the enemy prevents us from facing him/her squarely. Fear of the enemy troops across the country's border will prevent a soldier from performing his duty properly. Fear of the gun-toting criminal in the street of a city will prevent the local police constable from apprehending him. Fear of reprisal will make you weak and you will be unable to bring to book the powerful people who exploit you in various ways. Another example is when a female employee is afraid of losing her job because her superior or employer tends to exploit her sexually.

The world is full of friends with also a sizeable number of enemies. You have to be careful and circumspect in identifying the friend and the foe. You need to shed the fear of both. The world is witness to revolutions by people against oppression, exploitation and depredation by the ruling elite. The French Revolution, the Indian Mutiny of Independence and the American War of Independence were struggles of this kind. Such struggles take place when the element of fear is overcome.

Fear is the debilitating devil that destroys you. You have to get the better of it to advance in the tumultuous journey called life. Man is grossly limited of knowledge and understanding as against his/her Creator, who is omniscient. We don't know what dangers lie ahead of us in our life. There are known as well as unknown sources of danger to your life, wealth and property. If you harbour fear of those sources, you will not be able to lead a normal life. You will even be unable to properly perform your regular chores and important tasks. So, it is better to get rid of fear and take action to mitigate objectively the assessed risks in life. Fear of known objects can be removed by mitigating the risk emanating from those objects. But fear of unknown objects is entirely imaginary.

We can easily forgive a child who is afraid of the dark; the real tragedy of life is when men are afraid of the light.
—PLATO

For overcoming imaginary fears, you need divine help. Chanting of this fearlessness mantra on a regular basis enables you to do it. But since the mantra also addresses fear of known objects, the internal vibrations produced by chanting of this divine mantra also make you better equipped, both mentally and intellectually, to deal with dangers from known objects. This situation can be realized only if we are knowledgeable and not in illusion or delusion. By improving our mental focus and intellectual sharpness, this mantra aids in overcoming illusions of everyday life and fears born out of them.

When you have problems and issues with people at your school, college or workplace, you are likely to suffer pangs of fear of the day. When you have night cramps, insomnia or a nagging cough that worsens at night, you will fear the night. This mantra addresses both types of fear. The divine power of the mantra works scientifically, not miraculously, to resolve your relationship issues with people you interact with during the day. Application of this mantra also shows you the way to successfully tackle your health problems, so that you get a good night's sleep.

The subtle, scientific power of this divine mantra serves to provide protection to you and your material assets dispersed all over. It has the power to protect you from dangers, accidents and disasters. It gives a protective shield, because the benevolent Creator wants you to live for one hundred years in sound health, while preserving and increasing your material assets. The all-powerful Creator wants to help you in leading a fulfilling life.

You only need to understand the desire of the divine Creator and take His help. Achievement of freedom from fear is no mean achievement. A person who has overcome fear has reached a stage of elevated existence from where no obstacle is insurmountable and no challenge is too difficult to meet. A fearless person boldly steers his/her life boat forward. He/she is victorious in all his/her ventures because the very absence of fear means that he/she is fully prepared, fully groomed, makes best efforts and has full faith in the justice of the Almighty. Further explained, the path to fearlessness enjoins upon a person to work with patience, honesty and true knowledge. It calls for perseverance and truthfulness and an approach that is in harmony with the surroundings.

It follows from the above that fear is antithetical to progress and to life itself. No one can progress in life without taking due calculated risks, as the charm of life lies in action, not in material rewards of those actions. Happiness, which every human mortal seeks, is a journey, not a destination. And this journey can be pleasing, charming and rewarding only when undertaken without fear. Hence fearlessness is an important ingredient of right action. i.e. action that inevitably leads to happiness and fulfilment. Success comes unfailingly—sooner or later, when fear is overcome. Vanquishing fear is essential to progress and spiritual transcendence of man.

Regular chanting of this mantra too gives exactly the results sought in this mantra. It builds your character so that you are able to meet challenges posed by your enemies and also the expectations of your friends. It gives you the courage to counter the fear of known objects and develops an innate sense of security against unknown objects, the latter through strengthening of faith in the divine protector. It improves your physical and mental health so that you feel comfortable during the day and sleep well at night. It gives you divine protection from all other dangers and threats.

Epilogue

Challenges related to health, security and sustainability are widespread in today's world.

But life moves on. Pleasure and pain are an integral part of this life. No human worth his/her salt desires pain or sorrow of any kind. But they seem to be inevitable. Actually, pain and sorrow are avoidable. They stem from ignorance, inaction and improper action. We need to overcome our ignorance and get rid of the illusions that cloud our mind. For this, we need to understand a few simple facts. The first and the foremost is that we need to reconcile our limitations against the infinite capacity, infinite power and omniscience of our divine Creator. And the second is that we need to follow the knowledge base provided to us by the Creator for our peaceful and fulfilling eternal existence.

The world community never remains in the same condition. Things are dynamic and keep on changing every moment. Cycles of time come and go and vast changes and transformations are witnessed through decades, centuries, millenniums, ages and eons. The Creator as an animate, immanent power remains eternally with us and functions in a caring and guiding mode. We have to heed His guiding signals and move on. We have to tap the strands of knowledge of the Vedas to attain peace and happiness. We have to strive for it. Everything is within our reach—we only need to have a positive and realistic outlook and work for it. Sincerity, devotion and perseverance are the watchwords in this.

The present generation has to revisit the above

understanding and overcome the tendency to hedonism and monetary greed. The divine principles of healthy, sustainable and peaceful living will never change. We just need to keep ourselves aligned with them.

Acknowledgements

My heartfelt acknowledgements are due to the following persons for their invaluable contribution in the accomplishment of this work.

Members of the Arya Samaj, Vasant Kunj, New Delhi for their motivation and support, in particular Sh. Nirmal Kandhari, Patron; Com. P.C. Bakshi, President and Sh. Narendra Tuteja, Past Secretary.

My wife Smt. Bindu Sehgal, Principal, Delhi Public School (DPS), Vasant Kunj, New Delhi for her unstinted support in the pursuit of my passion.

The team of editors at Rupa Publications for their professional editing and embellishment of the manuscript.

I would also like to thank the production staff at Rupa Publications.